TORCH BIBLE COMMENTARIES

Amos and Micah

AMOS
AND MICAH

JOHN MARSH

SCM PRESS LTD

334 00040 8

First published 1959
by SCM Press Ltd
58 Bloomsbury Street, London WC1
Ninth impression 1979

Printed in Great Britain by
Fletcher & Son Ltd, Norwich

CONTENTS

5

11   1382

PREFACE

In sending this book to the publishers I would like to do
three things.

First, to acknowledge that I am, in common with all
those who set out to comment on the Bible, the most
wonderful treasure store in the literature of the world,
deeply indebted to those who have taught and written before. In particular I want to mention three to whose teaching
I owe more than I can say: to Duncan Cameron, who first
taught me Hebrew in the University of Edinburgh; to John
Naish, who helped me to begin to realize what a wonderful
storehouse the Hebrew Old Testament is, and what un-
searchable riches are in the prophetic books and the
prophets' nature; and to Professor Wheeler Robinson, who,
first as teacher and later as a revered senior colleague, set
standards of work and scholarship that will remain always
beyond my attainment.

Second, to thank the SCM Press, and Ronald Gregor
Smith and David Paton in particular, for their great
and tolerant patience with a tardy writer, and to
express the hope that this volume will not betray their
trust.

Third, to say that I have had the ordinary layman in my
mind throughout, and the world he lives in. I have used, as
I was asked, the Authorized Version as the basis of my
remarks, and I have tried to make that text 'come home'
to the twentieth-century reader.

I hope and pray that this commentary and all the others in the Torch series will help twentieth-century Christians to become again a Bible-reading people.

JOHN MARSH

Mansfield College,
Oxford
November 1958

GENERAL INTRODUCTION

PROPHECY AND THE PROPHETS

Not least among the benefits of the modern study of the Bible has been a new insight into the life and work of the prophets of the Old Testament. Amos, whose book we are to consider, has been frequently called 'The first of the great prophets'. In a sense he was; but if we try to see exactly how true and how false that description is, we shall have gone a long way towards understanding what prophecy meant to the Old Testament people of God, and what a prophet really was.

Amos began to prophesy about the middle of the eighth century BC, and, in reading the book which bears his name. it is easy enough to see why the earlier representatives of modern biblical study came to think that something quite new came into Hebrew history, and indeed human history, with his prophesying. If we turn back to the earlier strands of Old Testament narrative, the picture of prophecy that is painted for us seems radically different from that which Amos represents.

One day, some 250 years before Amos, Saul was sent to find his father's lost asses, and we read that after a long and fruitless search Saul proposed to return home. At that point his servant said to him: 'Behold now, there is in this city a man of God, and he is an honourable man; all that he saith cometh surely to pass: now let us go thither; peradventure he can shew us our way that we should go.' So

they go to Samuel, who tells them that the asses have
already been found. In an aside put into the narrative
the writer says that Samuel was a prophet, though in earlier
times he would have been called a seer. There are two
points to be noted in the conception of prophecy embodied
in this story: the prophet was thought to be the right person
to consult as to the whereabouts of lost property; and he
was supposed to be able to foretell the future. Neither of
these faculties are very acceptable to modern man, and it
is worth noting that Amos was not, so far as we know, a
person who set up as a clairvoyant for consultations about
lost goods; nor does his prophecy contain the sort of prediction of the future that lies behind the statement of
Saul's servant about Samuel's powers. Prediction there may
be in Amos, but it is of a kind radically different from
that of a seer who foretells the finding of lost animals, or
is able to report it by virtue of his occult powers.

But the story of Saul can take us further in our knowledge and understanding of the history of prophecy. When
Samuel sent Saul back to his home with the news that his
father's asses had been found, he also told him that on his
way home he would meet a band of prophets and prophesy
with them. The story goes on: 'And when they came
thither to the hill, behold a company of prophets met him;
and the Spirit of God came mightily upon him, and he prophesied among them' (I Sam. 10.10). We know that such
companies or 'schools' of prophets were not uncommon
at the time of Elijah (about 850 BC), who, on the day that
he was taken up in a chariot of fire was met, along with
Elisha, by some of the 'sons of the prophets' at Bethel
and Jericho (II Kings 2.3-5). We know also that Ahab
kept four hundred prophets attached to his court (I Kings
22.6) and that they could either utter oracles together

vocally (I Kings 22.6) or make their predictions known by
the symbolic action of one of their number (I Kings 22.11,
where Zedekiah ben Chenaanah made horns of iron and
said, 'With these shalt thou push the Syrians, until thou
have consumed them '). Altogether we can piece together a
fair picture of this type of prophecy, where schools of
prophets could be kept or used for consultations, which
were often made in some sort of induced ecstasy (music,
dancing, singing, cutting of the body, incantation etc., cf.
I Sam. 10.5; I Kings 18.25 f., 28).

Amos and Micah showed a marked contrast with
prophecy of this sort. They were 'lone wolves', not members of a 'school'; Amos says of himself: 'I was no
prophet, neither was I a prophet's son; but I was an herdman, and a gatherer of sycamore fruit' (Amos 7.14).
Though they have visions, and speak of 'seeing' the word
of the Lord, there is no evidence at all that these visions
were induced by any of the professional 'aids to oracular
prophecy'; on the contrary, all the evidence we possess
points the other way.

Our two prophets thus do not find their predecessors in
the schools of the prophets which dominated popular and
national religion in the time of Ahab. Such 'schools'
of prophets were but the Hebrew counterpart to the sort of
prophet known among Israel's neighbours. (Beside the
prophets of Yahweh at Ahab's court there were upwards
of four hundred prophets of Baal kept for his foreign wife,
Jezebel.) If our two prophets had a forerunner—and it is
safe to presume that they were not entirely 'new'—he must
be sought not in a member of a prophetic school (unless
Micaiah ben Imlah be counted a member of a school;
though if he were, he was a very independent and contrary
member!) but rather in the persons of Elijah and Elisha,

who, a century before, had been acting as individually
called and appointed prophets of the Lord.

When the ministries of Elijah and Elisha are examined,
it is plain that their aim and purpose was to restore to an
Israel tempted to embrace the new gods of a newly met
and adopted culture, the undefiled religion that the people
had learnt in, and preserved from, their days in the desert.
Under the rule of Omri's dynasty (Omri 887-Joram 841) the
people of Israel had experienced what we should recognize
nowadays as a considerable economic and cultural trans-
formation. The task of bringing a once nomad people to a
secure urban life, some once pastoral tribes to the complex
structure of production and exchange, was carried out with
rapidity and vigour and almost complete success by Omri
and his sons. The difficulties came in what seemed to the
' advance' party the residual religious adjustments that the
new life involved. As nomad learnt from settler the art of
rural economy he learnt that abundant crops were the gifts
of the local gods or *baalim*. As victor intermarried with
vanquished the gods of both spouses were accepted in the
one new home. As an expanding national economy found
its prosperity sealed and furthered in marriage alliances
with militarily stronger states, so into the royal palace and
into the royal shrine the foreign queen's god, Baal, was
introduced and supported in worship. Elijah had vision
and insight enough to see that along such paths the nation
would lose its unity and its integrity; and he fiercely
opposed not only the scandalous behaviour that the greed
of a new commercial economy occasioned, but also the
whole range of religious action that in any way detracted
from the worship which he believed belonged solely to God,
to God who had been with them in the desert, and had
both brought them out of Egypt and its slave ghettos, and

led them into their new territory and prospered them in it.

Elijah was thus the first great prophet to see clearly the issues that confronted the Mosaic religion that the Hebrew tribes had brought in from the desert, as it was put to the test of survival in a new culture. There were, of course, other voices. There were those who looked hopefully to the new gods of Canaan or of Tyre, and believed that the future lay with them. Elijah was involved in a tremendous battle with these seducers of Israel on Mount Carmel (I Kings 18.20-46). But in their own day these doubtless constituted the party of progress and cultural 'advance'! There were also those who practised, as they pleaded for, a retention of all desert customs in reaction against the influence of the new Canaanite and Tyrian cultures. These were the 'Rechabites' who still dwelt in tents and abstained from wine (cf. II Kings 10.15 ff.; Jer. 35.6-10). Elijah represents a 'middle way', neither adopting the religion of the new culture, nor yet rejecting the culture wholly because of its alien religion, but pleading that the pure religion that Israel had learnt from Moses in the desert should remain the true spring of Israel's nationhood in the new culture, as in the old.

Amos and Micah lived in times not dissimilar from those of Elijah and Elisha. In their day Israel was prosperous, indeed the northern kingdom never had more prosperous times than under Jeroboam II, in whose reign Amos preached, and Judah had also savoured commercial expansion and advance. In their day, too, the surrounding great powers became the cause of the adoption of alien forms and symbols of worship; and in their day, too, the story of Naboth's vineyard was repeated in the pitiless expropriation of many a helpless peasant, the unhappy victim of drought or blight. To their day, as Elijah and

Elisha before them, they preached a renewal and revival
of Mosaic religion. It was this religion that had made out
of many tribes one people, that had given them a political
unity and a social stability, that had given them a monarchy
neither absolute nor tyrannical, but itself subservient to
God, and open to censure from prophet and priest, that had
given them morals and a morale unapproached elsewhere
in the ancient east, and a religion and a ritual unsurpassed
in its purity and spirituality. The work that Elijah did in his
day as a reviver of Mosaic religion, Amos and Micah
continued in theirs, relative to their own circumstances.
The chief characteristics of their work we shall see.

But this brief review, starting from the conventional
modern judgment that Amos was the 'first of the great
prophets of Israel' has led us back, significantly, to an old
biblical judgment. The Book of Deuteronomy ends with
the story of the death of Moses, and relates how all Israel
mourned for him. The book closes: 'And there hath not
arisen a prophet since in Israel like unto Moses, whom the
Lord knew face to face; in all the signs and the wonders,
which the Lord sent him to do in the land of Egypt to
Pharaoh, and to all his servants, and to all his land; and in
all the mighty hand, and in all the great terror, which Moses
wrought in the sight of all Israel.' This is a view of prophecy
with which our two prophets would wholeheartedly agree.
What they 'saw' of God did not originate, they would
say, with themselves; they saw what they did only by standing in the great tradition of the revelation given to Moses
long before. It was on the basis of an appeal to that earlier
revelation that the 'word of the Lord' which came to Amos
and Micah had real validity (cf. Amos 2.10; 3.1 f.). It was
ultimately from Moses that both prophets derived their
monotheism. It was Moses who had first taught the doctrine

that was now the basis of their own prophetic preaching, that the unity of the tribes that had come through a confederacy to be one people rested in the end upon a divine choice, calling and constitution that they should become the people of God. And it was from Moses that they received what seemed in the eighth century a new emphasis—the insistence that religion, if real, meant morality and social justice as well. Moses had, according to the tradition they inherited, taught them about the God they worshipped, the one God, who was Lord of all creation and of all history. It was Moses who had been their representative and had enacted on their side the covenant relationship which stamped them as his people. It was Moses, who had taught them monotheism, who also taught them of the consequent duties to their neighbours, and demanded a just order in the then more primitive society. Here, in the eighth century, we are able to witness the flowering of Mosaic religion, and in the biblical sense, of Mosaic prophecy, in the work of Amos and Micah.

Of Moses' call we have some record. Of the call of Amos and Micah we know almost nothing. Amos says nothing save two things: First, 'The Lord took me as I followed the flock, and the Lord said unto me, " Go, prophesy unto my people Israel ".' And secondly, 'Shall a trumpet be blown in the city, and the people be not afraid? Shall there be evil in a city, and the Lord hath not done it? . . . The lion hath roared, who will not fear? the Lord God hath spoken, who can but prophesy? ' Evidently there was something infinitely compelling about the vocation of a prophet. We do not know how it was that Amos and Micah were able to receive and then to revive the purity of Mosaic religion, and fashion it to the demands of a new era. Nor do we know in what form the pressure of God came. We do know that each of them found it irresistible, whatever the cost might be. Perhaps the words of a modern poet will help us to enter imaginatively into the prophetic vocation, remembering all the time that in biblical religion no experience of God can be separated off from history and tradition, however critical the mind inspired by that experience may prove to be. Pushkin writes:

> With fainting soul athirst for Grace
> I wandered in a desert place,
> And at the crossing of the ways
> I saw the sixfold Seraph blaze;
> He touched mine eyes with fingers light
> As sleep that cometh in the night:
> And like a frighted eagle's eyes,
> They opened wide with prophecies.
> He touched mine ears, and they were drowned
> With tumult and a roaring sound:
> I heard convulsion in the sky
> And flights of angel hosts on high,
> And beasts that move beneath the sea,
> And the sap creeping in the tree.
> And bending to my mouth he wrung
> From out of it my sinful tongue,
> And all its lies and idle rust,
> And 'twixt my lips a-perishing
> A subtle serpent's forked sting
> With right hand wet with blood he thrust.
> And with his sword my breast he cleft,
> My quaking heart thereout he reft,
> And in the yawning of my breast
> A coal of living fire he pressed.
> Then in the desert I lay dead,

> And God called unto me and said:
> ' Arise, and let My voice be heard,
> Charged with My Will go forth and span
> The land and sea, and let My Word
> Lay waste with fire the heart of man.'[1]

For two prophets from a background of pastoral and agricultural life, sensitive on the one hand to the glory and majesty of God's transcendent holiness, and on the other to the inhuman sinfulness of man, this poem is perhaps the proper descriptive introduction. For only in some such experience could they have found the ability to utter in confidence and humility, in resignation and hope, in warning and promise those searching, judging yet ultimately healing oracles which began so significantly with ' Thus saith the Lord '.

THE MAKING OF A PROPHETIC BOOK

The last hundred years or so have seen some remarkable changes in our understanding of how a prophetic work came into being. A hundred years ago most readers of the Bible, even serious scholars, would have supposed that if a book were inscribed ' The Book of the Prophet Amos ' then the whole of the book as it appeared in the Old Testament had first been spoken, and then written down, by the historical person called Amos.

But when scholars were provided with the tools of literary and historical criticism, this conception underwent considerable, if not violent modification. It soon appeared,

---

[1] ' The Prophet ', from *Russian Lyrics*, translated by Maurice Baring, Heinemann, 1943, p. 1.   Quoted by permission of the translator's executrix.

for example, about the Book of Amos, that some of it was
highly unlikely to have been spoken by Amos or anybody
else living in the eighth century BC. Various reasons were
given for this judgment. Some were linguistic: words
derived from some recognizably late source were to be
found in some parts of the book, and could not therefore
have been written by the historical Amos. Some were historical: some of the things said in the book presupposed
historical, political, social or religious conditions that were
non-existent in the eighth century BC, and these could not
have been written by the historical Amos. Some were
frankly theological: ideas that were not current in the time
of Amos, or that were wholly out of keeping with his own
manner of thought, could not be thought to have come from
him. Thus it was held that because Amos was overwhelm-
ingly a prophet of doom he could not possibly have been
the author of the last passage of the book; he was not the
sort of man who could write such a ' happy ending '!

Different though these two approaches to the problem of
the making of a prophetic book are, they share one thing
in common. They tend to think that the question which
the critic has to answer is the question about the alleged
authorship of the book by the person named in the title.
The older view accepted the ascription somewhat un-
critically; the newer view rejected it critically. It was not
surprising that in the popular imagination this debate should
have seemed to be about the authenticity as well as about
the authorship of various parts of the Old Testament.
Among ordinary people the work of the critic, sound and
valuable though it might be, was somewhat suspect; not
always, be it admitted, without some justification.

In the twentieth century new considerations have come
into view, which have radically changed the whole setting

of this debate, and offer a new and positive approach to the problems of authorship and authenticity. Without seeking to recount the way in which the new ideas have been generated and developed, or going into details of what they assert, we may say that the present situation in the understanding of the genesis of a prophetic book is something like what follows.

Each prophetic book has its origin in the spoken word of some named prophet. But it has been wrong to conceive the problem in terms of the relation of the whole book to that one historical figure. Biblical scholars should have been aware of this all the time, for we know enough of the prophetic ministries of Isaiah and Jeremiah to realize that the prophet of the Lord was not an absolutely solitary figure. In particular it would seem that the actual writing down of prophetic oracles involved the use of a disciple or circle of disciples (cf. Isa. 8.16; Jer. 36 *passim*). If we further ask ourselves how prophecies uttered by Amos and Micah in the eighth century BC were preserved until they were incorporated into the body of prophetic writings known as the Roll of the Twelve, certainly not earlier than the fifth century BC, and possibly as late as the third, the answer that is now seen to be much nearer the probable actual situation is that the written records of the spoken oracles of each canonical prophet were preserved by a continuing circle of disciples. In the process of preservation a number of things happened to them. The oracles themselves might be related to some historical occasion other than the one which prompted them, because, in the view of the disciples of a later day, the word of their master was pertinent still. Moreover, further oracles might well be added, if these seemed to represent in a new situation the fundamental teaching of the original master. An under-

standing of this kind makes the whole question of authorship and authenticity take on quite new proportions. The
question we need to ask is not 'Did Amos say exactly
this? ', but rather 'How can we best understand the deposit
of the tradition of Amos' teaching as it has come down to
us, preserved with loving care, from the hands of his disciples over many years? '

I have taken occasion in the body of the commentary to
point out on occasion how much this understanding of the
formation of our two books helps us to understand them
today. We can get some sense of the way in which the words
of the master remained for the disciples of later times a
living and authoritative Word of the Lord, illuminating
later situations with as much power as they had done at the
first. We can observe how they could adopt later sayings
by others of their circle as really nothing more than an
extension of their master's insight into their own lives.
The Book of Amos (or Micah) then is not, nor was it ever
meant to be, simply the record of what one man spoke on a
particular occasion in history; it is rather the deposit of a
tradition of 'Amos-prophesying' treasured in an 'Amos-
community' for many many years, finding itself patient of
constantly renewed application, and thereby proving to the
faithful disciples of Amos that the words of their master,
and the words that his spirit quickened in them, were verily
a Word of the Lord.

If this be the way to understand the formation of a
prophetic book, the commentator can see his task more
clearly. He is no longer concerned, because he is no longer
able, to make sharp distinctions between 'genuine' and
'non-genuine' oracles. Rather he will see the whole book
as a deposit of a tradition stemming from the person of the
prophet himself, and retaining through the centuries a

treasured relevance among his disciples. It may well be that even the material most clearly deriving from the historic situation of the prophet himself has undergone some modification; it will surely be the case that even the most apparently ill-fitting additions from a later age were treasured for reasons which seemed good to the continuing community of the prophet's disciples. But the fundamental task of exegesis will not now depend upon a distinction between what is genuine and what is not, but upon a recognition that the whole book represents the authenticity of a long-lived tradition of the importance and authority of a particular prophet. Such an exegesis will be a long way from both the older conservatism and the more recent historicism; it will be, in the providence of God, as we hope, a contribution to the understanding of the unity of Holy Scripture both in regard to an individual book, and in respect of its relationships with the whole Bible, in both Old and New Testaments, which is in its own way the authoritative deposit of the long tradition of the Hebrew-Christian religion.

THE BOOK OF
AMOS

INTRODUCTION

THE REIGN OF JEROBOAM II:
782-743 BC

Jeroboam II came to the throne of Israel in 782 at a time
when the nation was engaged in a war of liberation against
the long continued domination of Syria. He was fortunate
enough to find Syria in eclipse. The rising power of
Assyria had already marked the end of Syria's greatness,
and Jeroboam's predecessor, Jehoash (797-782), had already
begun the process of liberation and reconquest of lost
territory, reclaiming several Israelite cities from Ben-Hadad
(II Kings 13.25). Jeroboam followed up these victories
successfully; so much so that the historian could say of
him that HE RESTORED THE COAST OF ISRAEL FROM THE
ENTERING IN OF HAMATH UNTO THE SEA OF THE PLAIN (II
Kings 14.25), and his kingdom came to be as extensive and
prosperous as it had been in the proverbial days of Omri.
After the early years of his long reign had been spent
extending and consolidating his territories, Jeroboam settled
down to a somewhat care-free policy of commercial and
economic expansion. He governed the main trade routes
from east to west and from north to south, and his merchant
princes were not slow to take advantage of the new era
of expansion to line their own pockets quickly and ruthlessly. Social changes took place with unimaginable rapidity,
brought about by the exhausting period of the Syrian war,
and by the cynical opportunism of the *nouveaux riches* in

expropriating the small peasant farmer whenever occasion presented itself, as it would, for instance, in a year of bad or mu ilated harvest. The Israel that Amos came to know was thus a state where large fortunes were being quickly made, great estates being developed, summer houses and winter residences being built in fabulous luxury for the wealthy, and where, at the same time, there was a quite new class of poor, who were virtually, and sometimes actually, slaves of their rich landlords.

No doubt there was underground discontent. Outwardly however, the national life showed all the marks of a buoyant, optimistic economy. The optimism may appear quite understandable at a time when Israel had at last shaken off the hated Syrian yoke, but it was fundamentally and culpably short-sighted. It was plain beyond misconception that Syria's yoke had been cast off only because a far greater power was making a bid for the world domination. No true statesman could have failed to see that even if Assyria were temporarily hindered from advancing farther west she would advance into Palestine at the earliest opportunity with a force against which Israel would be practically helpless. But the rulers of Israel were blind, and they sensed no danger. Their blindness was in its essence a moral and spiritual defect, and it was Amos, the prophet from Judah, who made that incontestably plain.

The work of Amos then, belongs to that period of Jeroboam's reign when the Syrian war was over, the economy expanded, and the upper classes insensitively confident. In 745 BC Tiglath Pileser ascended the throne of Assyria, and at once the situation became menacing. It would therefore seem most likely that the work of Amos was done somewhere between 770 and 750 BC. That seems as near as we can get to an actual date. Amos' own (or his editor's) TWO

YEARS BEFORE THE EARTHQUAKE was doubtless of value once, but is of no use to us now.

AMOS THE PROPHET

Amos, we are told, was a HERDMAN; but the Hebrew word used to give that piece of information is not that normally used for a shepherd, but one implying that the person concerned was a 'sheepmaster', and the inference is that he owned his own flocks, and, as we learn later in the book, also had a business interest in growing SYCAMORE FRUIT, which he also harvested himself. He thus appears as a man of some little substance, but not, by any standards wealthy; the kind of person who in the modern world might run a smallholding, with a side-line as an additional source of income. If we may make one further deduction from the word used in 1.1 to describe Amos' occupation, it is that the kind of sheep envisaged by the word were well-known for their wool. This may serve as a reason for Amos' travelling to the centres of trade in the Northern Kingdom to sell the wool, instead of remaining in Judah and seeking to sell his wares in Jerusalem. In Israel he would be much more likely to find customers, and to get higher prices. So we may conceive of Amos' life as shepherd and fruit farmer being interrupted at the time of the great seasonal markets, when he would go to one of the commercial centres of Israel. The time of his visits would always coincide with some great religious festival.

What Amos saw moved him deeply. Although like a good southerner he held the northern kingdom responsible for the political and religious division of the people of God, he could not but agonize for them in the condition in

which he found them. Prosperity was there in plenty: great
fortunes were being made; trade flourished and commerce
grew. The new class of rich left noticeable signs of their
prosperity: fabulous town houses with ivory-inlaid furni-
ture; banquets with wine and women and song; summer
residences in the cool hill country; the adoption of
'civilized' fashions for the women. They also left signs
of their religion—or better, their religiosity. Religion
flourished. Grand shrines were built and priests maintained
to serve at them. Sacrifices were offered, and the wealthy
paid their tithes proudly. The great festival services were
impressive and well attended. But they also left notable
signs of their basic irreligion, in callous and unjust treatment of the poor; in pitiless exploitation of the peasant
farmers' misfortunes; in purchasing the verdict of the
courts and the blessing of the priests by systematic and
extensive bribery. This was irreligion, because no man
could really meet with and worship the Holy God of the
true Israel and be involved in such injustice and oppression.
Worship therefore could be no more than a ritual per-
formed; it could not be a real confrontation between a
holy God and a sinful people.

We do not know the circumstances of Amos' call as we
know about the call of Isaiah and Jeremiah. But I have
suggested in the commentary that the section 7.1–8.3 forms
an account of a particular year in the life of the prophet
which is as near to an account of a call as we can get. The
section includes the story of the rejection of Amos at Bethel,
presumably located at its chronological position in the story.

But while we know nothing certain about Amos' call,
we know clearly enough what he was called to say. Basically it can be reduced to an appeal to Israel to realize
that the religion they had brought in from the desert did

not belong simply to the nomad life; it must be given free course in the new and exciting commercial and cultural advance. Israel, understandably, tended to accept, with the commerce and culture she was borrowing and learning from her neighbours, the religion that accompanied it. But this was not a true religion, for it was a religion of rites and ceremonies, making no demands upon the moral obedience of the worshipper. Personal sin and social oppression could easily be practised by the devotees of these cultic faiths. But Amos reminded Israel of her roots in Mosaic religion, and of the righteous covenant that God had made with his people in his love for them. God is presented again to his people as the living, loving and righteous God.

At a time when, in a new development of the agricultural arts, Israel would be taught about the influence of nature deities upon the crops, Amos reasserted the Mosaic belief in Yahweh as the God of nature, the God who sent the earlier and the later rains, the God who also RODE UPON THE STORM; who gave crops, or sent famine; a God who could not be used by man for man's purposes, but a God who required men to be obedient to the divine purpose. At a time when Israel was beginning to learn, from her growing international contacts, that every nation had its own god, and that it would therefore pay a weak nation to offer some respect to the gods of stronger neighbours, Amos asserted the claim that all the nations were under the judgment of Yahweh. He was Lord of history, as of nature. He was not a being who could be used and calculated on in the working out of international relationships; rather was he the God whose will was above all nations, using them for his own purposes, even when they flouted his laws. At a time when it appeared that it was quite safe to do injustice to achieve a large fortune, because the judges

could be 'squared' to return a favourable verdict in any
court case, and the priest could be paid to offer sacrifices to
'square' the deity, Amos taught that God could have
nothing to do with such evil—save to condemn it to the
destruction it deserved. This inevitably produced a note of
'doom' in the prophecy of Amos, and he has often been
called the prophet of doom. But, basically understood,
Amos is a prophet of God's caring, of his love, patience
and mercy; of a God who really cares what happens to
his people, and what they become, who will resort to any
necessary discipline in order to save them from themselves
and from the evils of the world. No one would say that
Amos comes with a full Christian understanding of God;
but none with spiritual discernment will fail to detect in
him a great forerunner of the Word incarnate, who saw
men's relationship to himself as the decisive factor, deter-
mining whether they should perish or have everlasting
life. To preach the God of real, active love, of love potent
in history, is at times, as Amos reminds us, to speak words
of rebuke and condemnation. If God cared less, if Amos
had been less sensitive to his word, we might have had a
'pleasanter' book, but it would not have spoken, in that
situation, of God's infinite and patient love.

OUTLINE OF AMOS

I

THE UN-ISRAELITE SERMON: 'FROM CIRCUMFERENCE TO CENTRE'

1.1–2.16

II

SERMONS OF DOOM

3.1–6.14

III

SERMON MATERIAL: A SERIES OF VISIONS IN A 'WONDERFUL YEAR'

7.1–8.3

IV

FURTHER SERMON MATERIAL

8.4–9.10

V

EPILOGUE:
EVENTUAL RESTORATION

9.11-15

COMMENTARY ON AMOS

I

THE UN-ISRAELITE SERMON:
'FROM CIRCUMFERENCE TO CENTRE'

1.1–2.16

Whatever be the relationship between the words that the
historic Amos uttered and the opening section of this book,
two things can be stated with fair confidence. First, that
standing at the beginning of the book, it is meant to offer
the reader a characteristic sample of Amos' preaching; and
second, that since it was the prophet's preaching that got
him into trouble with the Israelite authorities at Bethel,
this section gives us the sort of sermon which Amos
preached on that occasion (7.10-17).

The form of the sermon is excellently adapted to its
function. Imagine the Judean prophet standing in the market and cathedral square of the Israelite city and launching
forth on a series of denunciations of Israel's enemies,
threatening them with divine retribution for their ruthless
inhumanities and injustices. Imagine the excitement of the
crowd growing as the foreigner denounces the oppressors of
Israel one after another: watch the astonished applause
when he pleases the Israelite crowd most with a fierce exposure of his own country's improper attitude to the law
—the very charge that a Judaean normally laid against

Israel. Hear, finally, first the amazed silence, and then the
angry outcry against Amos, when he comes to the perora-
tion of his sermon: FOR THREE TRANSGRESSIONS OF ISRAEL,
AND FOR FOUR, I WILL NOT TURN AWAY THE PUNISHMENT
THEREOF. No wonder the authorities had to keep Amos
from making any further disturbance at the feast! The
courage of a Judaean trader at the festival market, in de-
nouncing the people whose separation from Judah was the
cause of unparalleled bitterness, was amazing; and nothing
less than his own explanation of it is adequate (cf. 3.3-8).

THE MAN WHO PREACHED

1.1 f.

1. Amos of Tekoa (for that is the better order) was **among
the herdmen.** Tekoa is about twelve miles south of Jerusalem, about 3,000 feet above sea level, looking eastward
towards the Jordan Valley, the Dead Sea and, beyond, the
mountains of Moab. The pasturage is scanty, and Amos
had to cover a wide area to keep his flocks in good pasture.
The Hebrew word for HERDSMEN is an unusual one, and
tells us something of the prophet's trade, for it was used
of the sheep farmed principally for their wool, and it was
probably in the first place as a wool merchant that Amos
went to the Israelite trade fairs at Bethel and other shrine
cities.

The words of Amos . . . which he saw. Note the combina-
tion of vision and speech so characteristic of the great
Hebrew prophets. Their visions were private. but words
gave them universality and permanence.

Uzziah (or Azariah) reigned in Judah from 789 to 739,
and Jeroboam II in Israel from 782 to 743. The earthquake
is of no use now, though it was at one time, in giving a
more precise date. All that can safely be said is that what
Amos says presupposes that Israel was not, and had not
been for some time, involved in war. Therefore Amos
could not have prophesied in the early years of Jeroboam's
reign, during which Israel was winning back the last
of her territory from Syria (II Kings 14.25); the most
likely date for his prophecies would therefore be about
760 BC.

The earthquake referred to clearly made a great impression on the Israelite community (cf. Zech. 14.5), and
on the sensitive spirit of Amos.

The prophecy opens with a kind of Introduction. Amos
(or possibly a later disciple) boldly states that he derives
his religious inspiration from Jerusalem, and that when the
God of Judah speaks even the mountains of Israel are as
much affected as Judaean pastures.

DAMASCUS

1.3-5. Now follows the series of denunciations of Israel's
enemies. Damascus (for Syria, north and east of Israel—
how often and how rightly the Hebrew prophet takes the
capital city as an epitome of the whole national life!) is
chided for an innumerable (the force of THREE . . . AND
FOUR) number of crimes—her conquering generals have
driven their iron-shod chariots over the prostrate bodies of
their prisoners of war. The retribution is a fire (i.e. a war)
that shall consume the whole state, including the royal
house (palace of Ben-hadad), the capital city (the bars of
Damascus were the iron bars to hold the gates firm against
attack), provincial governors (the sceptre holder of Eden—

where the Sun was worshipped); the whole people will be
taken captive and transported.

PHILISTIA

1.6-8. Gaza (for Philistia, south and west of Israel) has
been the centre of the slave trade, unto which they surrendered whole populations. Again, war shall overtake
them, governors and people alike.

TYRE

1.9 f. Tyre (for Phoenicia, north and west of Israel) had
also been a centre of the slave trade, but in her case the
offence was aggravated because she had sold Israelites into
slavery in spite of a treaty of friendship (brotherly covenant) between Hiram and Solomon (cf. I Kings 9.13; II Sam.
5.11; I Kings 5.1 ff.). A brief pronouncement of a destructive war suffices now to indicate the divine retribution
upon ruthless inhumanity.

EDOM

1.11 f. Edom (south and east of Israel) is condemned
because she turned against her most closely related people,
Israel, and treated her ruthlessly, without any remission at
all. Teman and Bozrah are important cities, used instead
of, and meaning, Edom itself.

AMMON

1.13-15. Ammon (east of Israel) had in savage attack (not
defence) practised the shocking cruelty of disembowelling
pregnant women. For this, war is to engulf their capital,
which shall itself hear the exulting shouts of an all-destroy-
ing invader. The whole royal house will go into captivity.

MOAB
2.1-3. Moab (south and east of Israel) has committed an act of desecration upon the remains of the king of Edom, for which sacrilege (typical, not isolated) war will destroy the kingdom and its rulers. Kerioth (or Ar) was the chief city (Isa. 15.1) and is described on the Moabite stone as a shrine of the god Chemosh.

THE FOE AT THE CENTRE
2.4 f. Judah (south of Israel). This is the unexpected, almost unbelievable utterance of the ' Sassenach' who has come north of the border, and now prophesies against his own nation, and gains even more popularity thereby. The charge against Judah is the very one which Judah lays against Israel—that they have rejected the sacred law, and have disobeyed it. No doubt this was more than mere rhetoric on the lips of Amos; in any case, in spite of the disruption of the kingdom after Solomon both Judah and Israel were often meant by either one of the terms. But rhetoric it was, and a device well calculated to create the greatest possible astonishment when the climax of the sermon came in the next section. So far the listening crowd had been asked to join in the easy and comforting pursuit of condemning others for their sins. Amos now asks them to do something very different, to condemn themselves.

THE CENTRE OF ALL ISRAEL

2.6-16

2.6-8. NATIONAL UNRIGHTEOUSNESS
It is typical of Amos that the first charge to be laid in the

actual situation into which he speaks is of social injustice,
in language that shows it up for what it is, near slavery, for
which other nations have already been condemned by the
unsuspecting market crowd. Amos here denounces the way
in which an inhuman creditor will sell, or take, his debtor
into slavery in order to discharge a small debt. Righteous
here means innocent, and implies that the debtors were not
fraudulent, but simply, by reasons of misfortune, unable for
a time to pay a debt which they did not repudiate. To
PANT AFTER THE DUST ON THE HEAD OF THE POOR is to want
to possess the poor man 'body and soul', the dust referred
to being that which is put on the head in mourning—not
even that must remain unconfiscated by the inhuman
nouveaux riches! TO TURN ASIDE THE WAY OF THE MEEK
marks the brutal severity which will not let the uncom-
plaining, God-fearing poor man continue in his difficult lot
without casting more misfortune upon him.

Next Amos denounces an offence repugnant to all ethical
religions—sacred prostitution, which, evil enough in itself.
is made worse in Israel by the reduction of what was, even
erroneously, a religious rite. to mere sexual gratification.
This is doubly to profane the name of Israel's God. A
further sign of the irreligion at the heart of Israel's religiosity is that when the well-to-do worshippers appear
before the altar they use unredeemed pawned garments to
sit on, products of their own financial oppression. and drink
there wine bought from fines and bribes paid by those who
have been condemned in an unjust legal practice.

2.9-11. GOD'S RIGHTEOUSNESS

In this section of his sermon Amos contrasts Israel's
social injustice and cruelty with God's unfailing good will.
God had destroyed their enemies the Amorites (the in-

habitants of Palestine before the Israelite invasion) and
had before that delivered them from oppression and injustice in Egypt, and disciplined them in forty years of
preparation for their life in the Promised Land. And to
keep them always reminded of their obligations to him God
had raised up prophets to proclaim his word, and Nazirites
to set an example of devout ' Puritan ' living. The Nazirites
were distinguished by not cutting their hair, and by ab-
stinence from wine; thus continuing, even after the settlement in Canaan, the simple yet adequate austerities of the
desert wanderings. By so doing they reminded the body of
the nation of the simplicity and integrity that were adequate
for real religion, which was imperilled by the wealth and
luxury of Jeroboam's prosperous reign.

2.12-16. THE DARKNESS AHEAD
In this final section of his sermon Amos makes two points,
(1) that in spite of all that God had done, Israel had
rejected him, and (2) that in consequence of this a severe
retribution was inevitable. God had given Israel the Puritan
Nazirites as a reminder of the austerities proper to a godly
society; but instead of learning from them Israel had made
them drink wine, and become indistinguishable from the
rest of the nation. And any people that thus destroys its
own idealists is in mortal peril. God had given Israel
prophets to speak his word and offer his counsel, but they
had been silenced by a nation too confident in its own
contemporary success to think it needed any divine
guidance. And any people that suppresses the truth is also
in dire peril.

It is important to notice, before we pass to consider the
first doom that Amos announces to Israel, that it was only
after God had done all that he could to win Israel's willing

obedience and trust, that Amos conceives him as willing ineluctable disaster.

But the disaster which is to be announced has, in the rendering of the AV, yet another antecedent. God himself feels the sin of Israel as a great burden (2.13), even if his people be unaware of it. It is for him like the weight of a fully loaded wagon at harvest time—and they have always been loaded as fully as men dared. God feels his people's sin and injustice as a great burden he must carry. How in the end he bore his people's sins is not known to Amos, though here is a perception that truly anticipates the Cross. (And if we substitute the RV text for the AV and so get rid of the idea that Amos knew that God felt the sins of his people, we cannot avoid the conclusion that this idea was known to Hosea [11.8 f.] and Isaiah [1.24], and it is therefore not a serious anachronism, if it is one at all, to suppose that Amos thought of God in this way.)

In the disaster that is to come the real adversary of Israel will be God. So it will be futile to seek to escape from the doom ahead. None will flee fast enough, nor have strength enough (2.14), nor shoot straight enough, nor be well enough mounted to effect escape from the destruction God will send (2.15). The courage of the bravest will desert him, and he will fly with the rest from the divine nemesis, with nothing (NAKED, 2.16) with which to protect himself from the retribution that God will send.

II

SERMONS OF DOOM

3.1–6.14

GOD'S PROPHET AND GOD'S PEOPLE

3.1-8

As an introduction to further 'sermons' of Amos we now
read a discourse which sets out two important underlying
conceptions—the fact of Israel's special relationship to God,
and its consequences when Israel was unfaithful, and the
fact and nature of the prophetic office as the means of communication between God and his people.

First, Amos has something new and startling to tell the
Israelites. God has something to say against them: they
are, as it were, criminals in the dock, and have to answer a
charge brought by the public prosecutor. And yet, having
begun by a clear statement of God's opposition to Israel,
the prophet characteristically and profoundly goes on to
address the people in terms of family intimacy: HEAR THIS
WORD WHICH THE LORD HATH SPOKEN AGAINST YOU, O
CHILDREN OF ISRAEL. Moreover, Amos reminds both
northern Israelites and southern Judaeans that they are still
one people in the sight of God, however sharp their human
divisions—THE WHOLE FAMILY WHICH I BROUGHT UP FROM
THE LAND OF EGYPT. The special relationship is of God's

making, not of Israel's choosing, and Amos confirms this
further by restating the popular nationalist theology of
his day: YOU ONLY HAVE I KNOWN OF ALL THE FAMILIES OF
THE EARTH. The word 'know' which Amos uses is the
verb used of a man's 'knowledge' of his wife in the in-
timacies of marriage, and he means to imply that Israel's
experience of God is likewise immediate and close. The
whole phrase means that such intimacy was not a universal
privilege, but a special gift. So far, at any rate at some
level, Amos would carry every one with him. But while
the hireling priest and prophet would say, 'You only have
I known . . . therefore I will preserve you from all the
dangers of the times,' Amos declares, YOU ONLY HAVE I
KNOWN . . . THEREFORE I WILL PUNISH YOU FOR ALL YOUR
INIQUITIES. It was this insight of Amos into the ways of
God with his people, which completely reversed the popular,
easy, superficial doctrine of the official priests and prophets,
that forms the basis of his minatory sermons. But while it
is important to remember the truth which Amos discovers
to his hearer, it is equally important to remember that the
judgments of God which he announces are to be under-
taken precisely because of God's intimate care for his
people.

Second, Amos, having said that he has uncomfortable
tidings to bring, speaks of the inevitability of the prophet's
word. It would appear that, like Moses (Ex. 3.11; 4.1, 10,
13) and Jeremiah (Jer. 1.6-10), Amos shrank from his unpopular duty, but found that he just could not keep silent.
If Israel heard a prophet declare the will of God, it could
be assumed that this was no chance affair, but a pre-
arranged act of communication, just as if Amos saw two
men walking together in the wild open country round Tekoa,
he could be sure that they had arranged to meet and walk

in company. Other inevitabilities from nature are used to
illustrate the inevitability of a prophet speaking the word
entrusted to him by God—a lion roaring means that he
has caught some prey, a roar in his den follows his capture
being taken home; if a bird is captured, a trap must have
been set for it. Then follow more pertinent illustrations,
bringing the matter nearer home: the bugle sound of
' alarm ' when the fierce bedouin make their raids always
strikes terror into the heart of the population. When a lion
roars, every one feels the fear. Just so, because God makes
his will known to his servants the prophets, once God has
spoken to the prophet the prophet must inevitably speak.

CORRUPTION AND INJUSTICE
IN ISRAEL

3.9–4.3

This sermon begins by the prophet making plain that
nations, like individual people, cannot do wrong ' on their
own '. If we think of God's dealing with his people's wrong-
doing in terms of a court of law, where God comes to lay
a charge against Israel, then, to keep the imagery, Amos
declares that the trial will be public. The Philistines and
the Egyptians—those ancient enemies who still wait for
signs of weakness in Israel in order to bring her into renewed subjection—will be present and interested parties.
They will learn of the rottenness at the heart of Israel, for
all its outward prosperity and deceiving show. Amos pictures them on the hills about Samaria, and sees them
watching the ruthless divine exposure of the conflicts going
on inside Israel and the oppression on which her prosperity

is based (3.9). The awful nemesis of the acquisition of wealth by unjust means is that men's consciences die— THEY KNOW NOT TO DO RIGHT.

11 f. The next painful duty of Amos is to indicate that the nations who thus are shown the moral weakness of Israel will themselves see an excellent opportunity for aggression. This will be the judgment of God upon the unjust society his people have built. Even if, in our sophisticated twentieth century, we may tend to see such action and reaction as part of the natural sequence of history, we may still acknowledge that it is God's will that has so ordered the reactions of peoples to one another in this world. The ruin produced will be complete—as complete as the destruction of a sheep caught by a lion in the Tekoan country, from which Amos saved on one occasion two legs, or, on another, only an ear. If 'Damascus' be the right trans- lation (the margin suggests 'the bed's feet'), Amos is reminding the Syrian people, as in the first sermon (1.3-5) that they cannot, any more than Israel, break God's moral laws with impunity.

14. Amos now selects three parts of Israel's national life that are inviting the destructive judgment of a God who cannot live with evil. First, the false religious life must go. The well decked altars of Bethel will be destroyed in the future invasion. The horns of the altar were used by fugi- tives as places of refuge—when a man caught hold of these his enemies could not harm him. Their destruction has a twofold significance—as symbols belonging to a corrupt society that offered no real refuge to the pursued man, they were to be destroyed as the unrealities they were; and as symbols of a refuge provided by God, their removal by

him was to indicate to Israel that the doom pronounced
by Amos could not be avoided.

15. Second, the imposing new social life would be destroyed. Some of the merchant princes of Israel had prospered exceedingly by their unrighteous oppressive principles
of trade. They had formed a class of *nouveaux riches* who
had both a winter house and a summer house. They had
built dwellings of the most costly materials to parade their
wealth; they had erected mansions to impress the world
with their greatness. They would learn soon that their
wealth was no more than a temporary security against the
extremes of climate, and that even the most solid mansion
could not stand when the judgments of God move in the
earth.

4.1 f. Third, the women who pitilessly egged their husbands on in their oppression and injustice would have to
bear their part of the divine retribution. Amos does not
spare them, for, like Isaiah, he sees that the quality of a
nation's womanhood is a fair index of its spiritual state.
The women share in their husbands' offences because what
they care about is not that justice should be done, but that
they should have their luxuries—WHICH SAY TO THEIR
MASTERS, BRING, AND LET US DRINK. Amos calls them KINE
(cows) OF BASHAN (east of the Sea of Galilee where there
was excellent pasture) who had taken up residence in
Samaria. Their well-fed, well-groomed appearance con-
trasted severely with that of the poor their husbands
oppressed. For their insensitiveness they would suffer, declared Amos. They themselves and their children would lie
dead in the streets, and, like the dead cows which they

would have seen, they would all be dragged away with
hooks to the rubbish heaps.

We may ask at the end of this sermon, where commercial
and city life has been ruthlessly condemned, whether most
of it is not due to the vivid life of a new city making its first
impression upon the simple naïveté of a lonely Judean
shepherd. No doubt Amos saw as clearly as he did because
of this contrast, but what he saw was not a mere social,
economic, or even, in the end, a moral problem. What he
saw was a people that had entirely forgotten God, in spite
of pretending to the contrary, a people who thought that
they could prosper as they pleased, and disregard the love
and justice of God. Amos has to warn them of this pro-
foundest peril.

THE RELIGIOSITY OF RELIGION

4.4 f.

This is too brief to be called a ' sermon '. But it may well
represent the sort of unit which Amos and other prophets
normally used, with its short form, terse language, and
poetic structure—all making it easy to remember. This
' sermonette' was evidently treasured as a satirical attack
upon the false and hollow worship of the Northern
Kingdom.

Come to Bethel (the royal shrine); Amos' hearers would
expect him to go on ' and worship God '; instead he says
TRANSGRESS. The injunction to sacrifice every morning and
to pay tithes every three years (the margin rightly suggests
that tithes were commanded every three days) is an appeal

to make every possible religious observance. To OFFER A thanksgiving SACRIFICE of leavened cakes was to burn it on the altar, the smoke being thought of as the means by which it was conveyed to God; to PUBLISH THE OFFERINGS needs no comment, save that it was an hypocrisy that Jesus himself condemned (Matt 6.1-4). Amos has exposed the incurable religiosity of the human heart. Even in a society built upon injustice and sustained by oppression the unjust oppressor will happily perform all the offices of religion— THIS LIKETH YOU, O YE CHILDREN OF ISRAEL, SAITH THE LORD GOD. But such a show, perhaps indistinguishable to the outward eye from real piety and love of God, is a hollow mockery, which God can only reject and destroy.

DIVINE WARNINGS IN THE PAST

4.6-13

In spite of very great differences, already apparent, between the religious insight and judgment of Amos and those of his Israelite audience, they shared some common convictions: that God was bound to Israel (as to Judah) by a covenant bond; that for this reason God would be concerned with the quality of Israel's life; that God had supreme power over both nature and history, and could (and would) use his power to discipline his people. The difference, of course, lay in the fact that while the people took their prosperity as a sign of God's favour and therefore of the satisfactory quality of their life, Amos saw in their oppression, sham religion, and widespread injustice a presage of doom. In this sermon he tries to illustrate his point by reference to the way God had dealt with them in

the past, and concludes with what might almost be called
a 'last appeal'.

Amos quotes five ways in which, as he believed, God had
been trying to discipline his people so as to get them to
return to him.

6. First, he has ordained famine.

I also is the translator's way of putting into English the
emphatic form of the first person singular pronoun. It is as
if over against the careless *nouveaux riches*, who thought of
famine as mere misfortune, God had said, 'Nothing of the
sort! These famines have been sent by me. They are my
handiwork!' Amos makes it plain that the object of such
action by God was not merely punitive or retributive, but
reformative and redemptive: God's comment on Israel's
reaction to his chastisement was: YET YE HAVE NOT RE-
TURNED UNTO ME. God, as all-powerful in nature, could and
did send famines; he had sent them as disciplines to Israel
in the hope that Israel might be brought to a renewal of
her responsibilities to God; but Israel had refused, and
persisted in ignoring God's signs, and arguing from her
present prosperity to the acceptability of her life before
God.

7 f. Secondly, Amos reminds the Israelites of the experience of being without rain at a vital season of the year.
THREE MONTHS TO (i.e. before) THE HARVEST was the time
when the heavy seasonal rain should be falling, and unless
it did so fall (in February) there would be no chance of a
good harvest three months later: but God had made the
heavy rains to cease prematurely. This affected not only
the crops all over the land, but the water supplies of the

various cities. Some would experience drought because of
the drought in February; others with a more consistent
supply, would not be much affected. But harvest failure
and a lack of drinking water alike should have reminded
Israel of the chastisement of God. But neither did. Israel
remained contented and at ease, and 'did not return' to
the Lord.

9. Thirdly, Amos reminds his hearers of the devastating
effects of the hot, scorching wind from the desert, which
had produced blight and mildew in the standing corn. He
also recalls the destruction caused by plagues of palmer-
worm (=locust, which attacked the fig and olive harvest),
and again charges Israel with the complacent self-satis-
faction which kept them from turning back to God after his
kind and wise chastisements.

10. Fourthly, Amos reminds his northern neighbours that
they had suffered a pestilence as the Egyptians had suffered
before Moses had led Israel out of Egypt long ago. And
like Pharaoh, Israel had not turned to God. We cannot say
what the plague was, though as the rest of the verse refers
to war it was probably some disease arising from wartime
conditions. The loss of the country's youth, the capture of
its horses (war animals only at that time and place, and
equivalent to, say, tanks as distinct from cars in the
twentieth century) and the insanitary, revolting incapacity
to bury the dead before decomposition set in—all this
should have reminded Israel of its duty to God. YET YE
HAVE NOT RETURNED UNTO ME.

11. Fifthly, Amos refers to an earthquake that had already
worked a memorable destruction. He says that God has
overthrown some cities, as he had overthrown Sodom and

Gomorrah. The word ' overthrow ' is always used to describe
the destruction of Sodom and Gomorrah, and while the
important thing about that destruction is the theological
assertion that it was wrought by God, the form in which
men experienced it would be best expressed by reference
to an earthquake. Clearly this, as the climax of Amos' five
illustrations, was a disaster of great magnitude—it was a
miracle, as we should say, that there were any survivors at
all. Israel was like a brand plucked from the burning—
miraculously fortunate to have any existence left!

12 f. Having reminded Israel of the way God had dealt
with them already, Amos finally reminds his audience that
it is this same God with whom they still have to do, and
whom they must meet. He bids them, PREPARE TO MEET THY
GOD. This is not a threat of judgment, but a call to repentance. As if Amos had said, ' Don't let it have to be said
again, BUT YE HAVE NOT RETURNED TO ME, SAITH THE LORD,
but instead prepare to meet God. Repent; turn to him in a
new righteousness and a sincere worship.' For Israel does
wrong to suppose that God will not or cannot bring Israel
to book in the future in the same way as he has done in the
past. He is the God who made the mountains (how ancient
and immense he must be) and CREATED THE WIND (a God
invisible to man's eye), who can tell what men are thinking—even when they know not themselves (so he is like
the author of a novel, as twentieth-century imagination
might put it, with complete control of what his characters
do and suffer), who can produce an eclipse (TURN MORNING
INTO DARKNESS) and order the way of the thunderstorm
(TREAD ON THE HIGH PLACES). God, that is to say, has re-
sources of power at his disposal infinitely above man's; yet
he uses them all for man's good. Let Israel therefore prepare

to meet him in humility, repentance and a new obedience
in life.

THE DEATH OF A NATION

5.1-3

This 'sermon' is in the form of a funeral song for Israel
whom the prophet regards as dead. Amos says, THE VIRGIN
OF ISRAEL IS FALLEN, putting into the past tense something
that has not yet happened. This was a familiar device of the
prophets, to show how certain their forecasts were—as
certain as if they were speaking of something already past!
The word fall means to fall in battle, to die a violent death,
so that Amos is once more foretelling a military disaster
to a nation that thinks its prosperity secure. The word
'virgin' is full of meaning. Israel was like a young woman
betrothed to her future husband (God) before whose sad-
dened eyes she was cruelly slain, her body left with none
to care for it. This is put in another way in v. 3 where the
prophet forsakes metaphor for fact, and tells how there will
be 90 per cent. casualties to all the fighting men of Israel,
whether from large city or small village.

ISRAEL'S CRISIS AND GOD'S GRACE

5.4-15

This sermon, introduced like all the others in the section
by the phrase THUS SAITH THE LORD UNTO THE HOUSE OF

ISRAEL, is in three parts. The first is a call to seek God in
the crisis, the second deals with the crime and punishment
of a people, and the third with the hope of those who seek
God.

5.4-10. A CALL TO SEEK GOD IN THE CRISIS

The compilers of Amos' works had a fine sense of drama
when they followed the doom announced in 5.3 with the
other note, equally characteristic of Amos: SEEK YE ME
(God) AND YE SHALL LIVE. It continues, as the beginning of
another sermon, the idea at the close of the address in ch.
4, PREPARE TO MEET THY GOD. Seek him, meet him, and live.
That is the positive exhortation basic to all Amos' thought.
The implied negatives are then stated: Do not seek Bethel,
enter Gilgal or pass to Beer-sheba. The word translated
'seek' originally meant to ask for an oracle from some
diviner, and then to offer worship and obedience to God.
Amos contrasts the two meanings: 'Offer me true worship
and holy obedience and you shall have life of superabundant
quality. But true worship leading to real life cannot be
found if you go seeking oracles at Bethel, Gilgal or Beer-
sheba, where false priests, prophets and diviners pretend
to know and speak my will, but really know nothing of me,
being, like yourselves, sinful prisoners of a sinful society.'
The word LIVE is likewise full of meaning. It is not mere
length of days that Amos speaks of, not, therefore, simply
freedom from attack by armed invaders like the Syrians, or
from natural calamities like the earthquake, or from diseases
of the body like the plague, but a positive healthy ordering
of both private and public life in conformity with God's
righteous will, which is the only full and satisfying life for
men and states, a life which is related not only to the
passing phases of the temporal, but also to the abiding

realities of the eternal world. The fate of the false sanctuaries and their adherents will be that common to all temporal things—cessation, destruction, death; but the true
sanctuary, found not in such shrines but in true life before
God, is life more abundant and enduring. Amos calls for
repentance lest God BREAK OUT LIKE FIRE (5.6). Fire was the
familiar metaphor for war, and Amos is again foreseeing
the certainty of future military disaster unless the nation,
whatever its apparent advance into prosperity, regained its
moral and spiritual stature. A nation without morale cannot defend itself (5.6b).

Amos goes on to contrast the doings of unjust judges
and rulers with God's. God consistently pursues one holy
purpose; nothing can turn him aside from it. That is his
'righteousness'. But the false rulers and judges in Israel,
instead of constantly pursuing justice, and so achieving consistency, turn judgment to wormwood or bitterness (those
unjustly dealt with, usually because of their inability to
pay bribes, are bitter). That is their unrighteousness. Their
real duty is to seek the God of all constancy and consistency,
exemplified in his control of the stars (seven stars =
Pleiades), of day and night, and of the cycle of rain-river-
ocean-evaporation-cloud-rain. Such physical constancies of
God are but signs of his mind and spiritual consistency,
which, in pursuit of justice, will cause him to support the
oppressed poor against the wealthy exploiter, and when
that happens no show of power will prevent the execution
of God's redress. The evil at the heart of Israel's life is that
hatred has become the relationship between unjust judges
and the prophet of God. Naturally so, for he seeks to
abolish their evil traffic in bribes and injustices. Hence they
hate him when he rebukes them in the public court of
justice, the open place just inside the city at the gate; and

they hate him, and this is their condemnation, because he says what is right.

5.11-13. THE CRIME AND PUNISHMENT OF A PEOPLE

In this section of the sermon Amos addresses the wrong-doers, and tells them just what their iniquities are. They tread down the poor, exacting payment of debts in wheat when harvests are poor. From their gains they have built new houses out of mason-trimmed stone, a much more durable material than loose natural stones. But such durability will not enable them to stand in the day of God's judgment. The same will apply to their planting of vineyards.

12. After a plain statement of the gross perversion of civil justice the prophet says that if it were a mere matter of human prudence, he would, like others who see the injustice, keep silent. But, as we already know, when God speaks to his prophet, he *has* to break silence. THE LORD GOD HATH SPOKEN, WHO CAN BUT PROPHESY? (3.8).

5.14 f. THE HOPE OF THE GOD-SEEKERS

For all the apparent inevitability of doom, Amos dare not be wholly minatory. Even now a change of heart and life will bring its response from God. If the false prophets, who make play with the claim 'God is with us' (Immanuel), turn to God in sincerity and persuade the nation to HATE THE EVIL AND LOVE THE GOOD, AND ESTABLISH JUDGMENT IN THE GATE, then the worst catastrophes may, by God's favour, be averted. The issues for the nation are truly as large as life and death. SEEK THE LORD, AND YE SHALL LIVE.

THE EXPOSURE OF FALSE HOPES
AND FALSE RELIGIOSITY

5.16-27

16 f. At the beginning of this 'sermon' Amos returns to
the disaster which he sees ahead of an unrepentant Israel.
It will be a kind of universal funeral day, when in city
streets and rural ways alike ordinary folk and professional
mourners (an important part of any 'respectable' funeral)
will lament the death of the nation. God will pass through
Israel, as once he passed through Egypt; and though, on
that historic and fateful night Israel was spared destruction,
that will not be so in the doom to come.

By contrast, Amos scorns the false confidence of popular
religion. The common people had been taught to wait for
THE DAY OF THE LORD, and the picture had been attractively
painted in bright colours—Israel was to be 'top nation',
specially favoured and prospered by God. This was a false
and escapist religion, the leaders and rulers escaping from
the realities of international affairs, the oppressed poor
escaping from their inhuman treatment.

18-20. A true prophet had to burst this blasphemous
bubble. THE DAY OF THE LORD, the coming of God to his
people, could not bring an easy prosperity with no reckoning of Israel's worth. Rather would Israel's sin bring one
catastrophe upon another. The unjust rulers hoped that
the coming of THE DAY OF THE LORD would save them from
paying for their injustices in a rebellion, or for their unprincipled foreign policy in foreign conquest; the oppressed
poor looked forward to its arrival to bring them release

from human oppression, though without the costly moral and spiritual reformation that God required. In actuality, such hopes could only lead from disaster to disaster, like the flight of the man who ran from a lion into the way of a bear. Amos assured his hearers that when THE DAY OF THE LORD came, it would not turn out to be all sunshine, but, on the contrary, thick and impenetrable darkness.

21-4. Amos next traces the roots of these false hopes to religiosity parading as religion. Israel had all the externals of true religion—fine churches and cathedrals, great festivals popularly observed ('everyone went to church' on such days), moving rituals, solemnly impressive sacrifices, beautiful music and well-trained choirs. But such externals do not, of themselves, beget communion with God. Justice and righteousness, fair dealing and moral decency—these are indispensable conditions of any traffic between God and his people. In their absence, Israel's religion could only be 'religiosity'—the carrying out of rites and ceremonies for the 'good feeling' they evoke—it could not be a living encounter of a people with the God whose very nature was justice.

25-7. Amos appealed to the great, classic days of Moses, founder of Israel's religion. In the wilderness there had been no elaborate temple worship, and yet God had been with them. In v. 26 there is a reference to Israel's adoption of Assyrian Gods, and the translation should be: YOU SHALL TAKE UP SAKKUTH YOUR KING, AND KAIWAN YOUR STAR-GOD, WHICH YOU MADE FOR YOURSELVES. This adoption of Assyrian deities may not have been until Samaria had fallen, and if so, this verse probably derives from the treasury of Amos-like sayings preserved by the prophet's disciples.

The nemesis of this basically irreligious religiosity, which makes the whole nation suppose that it can sit loose to the demands of righteousness and integrity, will be, declares Amos, the conquest of Israel by Assyria, and the consequent captivity of the people. Nor is this simply a judgment of what seems an inevitability of history; it is fundamentally an assertion of the sovereign, judging, but redeeming activity of God.

THE FALSE CONFIDENCE OF INJUSTICE

6.1-14

This ' sermon ' is also meant to prick the bubble of a confidence based on a false religious outlook. It begins with a warning to those who, in their prosperity, are untroubled by their times. They are ' at ease in Zion ' (Amos thus includes his own nation, Judah, as part of the real unity of the People of God) and suppose that their military defences are adequate. These are the ruling classes, trusted by the people as political leaders and as judges (TO WHOM THE HOUSE OF ISRAEL COME), who like to think of themselves as great international figures.

Amos bids them remember that Calneh (Calno of Isa. 10.9 in North Syria), Hamath (on the Orontes) and Gath (in Philistia) had already fallen to the Assyrians; they must not suppose that Samaria could offer any more effective resistance than these. It is fairly certain that these three cities did not fall to Assyria until after Amos' time; thus we probably have a later prophetic saying of some disciple of Amos adapted to its present use because of its Amos-like quality.

The result of false confidence is to suppose that the day of reckoning is far off, even to think it non-existent, and to conclude that no reform of present injustices is necessary. The pitiless *nouveaux riches* assumed that their luxurious life would continue—ivory beds, improvident meat consumption, private orchestras, wine-bibbing, cosmetics etc.—and that the hard lot of the oppressed poor would persist unremedied. The worst of all was that they had no twinge of conscience about the national malaise.

The inevitable response of God to such cynical injustice would be to leave his people at the mercy of an invader. Israel might think her prosperity, and all the splendour (excellency) that displayed it, might make her valuable to God. But God saw the pomp and grandeur as signs of iniquity in the nation, and because no one in the nation would denounce them or reform them, God himself had to act (THE LORD GOD HATH SWORN BY HIMSELF), and Samaria, the man-made capital city, would be surrendered to an invader.

9 f. There is here an austere description of the conditions which will obtain during the siege. No family will be so large that it will not lose all its male members (v. 9), and when two odd survivors meet as they carry out the last rites for their dead, they will be so fearful of what God can do that they will be afraid even to speak his name (v. 10).

11. Here Amos uses the imagery of the earthquake (the word 'smite' is the same as is used in 3.15 and 9.1) to indicate the divine origin of the calamity which is about to overtake Israel. No one can suppose that an earthquake is

a human contrivance; the forthcoming catastrophe will be
as evidently a divine visitation.

12 f. The prophecy then turns back to consider the nature
of Israel's grossly unjust order. It is, says Amos, as unnatural as horses running on rocks or as a farmer ploughing
rock with his oxen. In Israelite society justice has turned
to bitterness, and all that a man can expect from righteous
living is economic and even personal extinction. Israel's
joy, instead of being in the eternal realities of justice and
goodness, is being found in what amounts to unreality,
nothingness. The reference to horns in v. 13 is to the pro-
tection afforded to fugitives from justice by the 'horns' of
the altar. The newly rich deem themselves to be in need of
no such support, thinking that the system they have devised
is its own security. (Alternatively, 'thing of nought' can be
transliterated 'Lo-Debar', a town where Mephibosheth was
for some years in hiding, and 'horns' can in the same way
yield 'Karnaim'. If these translations be adopted, the verse
is then directed against the blind self-confidence that
supposes two such small victories by Israelite arms can
guarantee security against Assyria's might.)

14. Finally, Amos adds a word to indicate the complete-
ness of Israel's coming destruction. The land will be overrun
by the invader, not only to the limits of its present boun-
daries, but to the farthest reaches of any territory it has
ever held. What is to be destroyed is not only contemporary,
empirical Israel, but the Israel of national memory and
pride, ideal Israel, as Israelites still wanted her to be.

III

SERMON MATERIAL: A SERIES OF VISIONS IN A 'WONDERFUL YEAR'

7.1–8.3

In this section is preserved the most personal information we have about Amos. We read of his decisive but unfruitful encounter with Amaziah, the priest at Bethel (7.10-17), and of a series of visions which, arranged as they are in their order of natural sequence, suggests that they all came to Amos in the same year as that in which he was deported from Bethel. The four visions are unique in this respect—that the basis of each is a public event or situation which everyone with two eyes could see; but what Amos saw was those same events and situations as indications of God's actions towards his people. He turned sight into insight, we might say.

THE FIRST EVENT-VISION: GRASSHOPPERS

7.1-3

The grasshoppers are really, as later translators have seen, locusts. The farmer who suffered from an invasion of locusts at the time of his first grass crop would doubtless grumble, but could look forward with hope to the second crop to recover some of his losses. But in this year of 'marvels' the locust invasion came with the ripening of the second crop, and everyone knew that nothing could be done to restore the situation. Amos saw this, not as an economic misfortune due to an accident of nature, but as a visitation by God (the force of THE LORD GOD SHOWED UNTO ME) indicating the certainty and the severity of the foreign invasion. The misfortune of nature was thus viewed as a kind of dramatized parable, telling sinful and unrepentant Israel of its impending doom. Though Amos knew, as Israel did not, the justice of such a divine visitation, he pleaded for the nation that his fellow countrymen in Judah mostly hated, and the Lord REPENTED. It does not therefore follow that God is changeable or capricious, but rather that he remains Lord of history. Nothing is certain 'on its own': everything happens according to his sovereign will and purpose. This is as significantly disclosed in the 'repenting' as in the threat of doom.

THE SECOND EVENT-VISION: FIRE

7.4-6

Later in the year of the locust invasion the summer grew excessively dry and hot. The sun seemed to be literally scorching up the earth, and even to have dried up THE GREAT DEEP, the huge volume of water which was thought to be beneath the earth, so that wells and spring dried up as well as the seasonal streams. Amos saw this second natural calamity as a picture of the destruction some enemy with a 'scorched earth' policy would work in the land; and again he pleaded for Israel. Again the Lord REPENTED—this was still not to be the final and decisive proclamation of doom.

THE THIRD EVENT-VISION: THE PLUMBLINE

7.7-9.

Later still, Amos was in Bethel, as we may suppose. He saw a good deal of new building going on—manifest sign of Israel's prosperity, and evidence of the security that was generally felt. It is tempting to imagine that it was at some new buildings for the royal temple at Bethel that Amos saw the wall being measured against a plumbline. He was one of many onlookers, we may be sure; but as he watched the craftsman at his work, the human picture faded and was replaced by something else: the wall had become Israel and the workman with the plumbline God. In the great deliverance under Moses, God had passed over, or passed by, his people of Israel; but now, Amos seemed to understand, God would pass by them no more; they would be measured as stringently as a wall is measured by a plumbline, which must be absolutely right, or it cannot be allowed to stand. And Amos knew and evidently made known his knowledge, that if God were so to measure his people, they would have to suffer destruction like an untrue wall. And the place of greatest weakness and error would suffer most —Israel's religious buildings, the high places in every town and village, and the sanctuaries or temples in the great centres of population.

'SO PERSECUTED THEY THE PROPHETS'

7.10-17

The activities of Amos during this year of many 'signs' could not pass unnoticed by the civil and ecclesiastical authorities. It is significant that the vision of the plumbline contains no plea for Israel by the prophet. It is a likely conjecture that the 'prophecy' was interrupted by the appearance of Amaziah, who could no longer be expected to remain inactive once Amos had foretold the destruction of Israel's ecclesiastical buildings.

Amaziah's charge of political conspiracy which he sent forward to the king, though quite false, was not wholly unnatural or malicious. After all, the existence of Israel as a nation separate from Judah owed almost everything to the prophet Ahijah; and even more clearly the establishment of the present dynasty on the throne was the work of one man—the prophet Elijah. The appearance of a Judaean prophet uttering menaces of invasion and destruction was a natural focus for political suspicion. And even without Israel's past history, the interpretation put upon Amos' conduct by Amaziah is one with that given to the work of Christian missionaries in many countries today, to the witness of the Confessional Church in Nazi Germany by the political bosses, to the reforming zeal of the early Congregationalists in Elizabethan England by the national church, or to the mission and ministry of Jesus by the Jewish leaders of his time. Yet even if political misrepresentation were understandable, Amaziah evidently overstated his case, imputing to Amos prophecies about the person of Jeroboam

that he had not uttered. Like many others in the course of
history, Amaziah played on the fears of another in order
to pacify his own.

12 f. Amaziah's statement to Amos is one demanding his
return to Judah. It claims (v. 13) to have royal authority
behind it, though perhaps the narrator means us to understand that it was assumed by Amaziah as the answer the
king would inevitably send to his report about Amos.

14 f. Amos' reply to the sentence of deportation is that,
unlike Elijah, he was not a professional prophet, still less,
unlike many whom Elijah saw on the day of his ascension,
was he a member of a prophetic guild or school. Had he
been, the conscience-stricken authorities might have had
excuse for repatriating him, for the prophetic guild had
before this proved a hot-bed of political revolution. Amos
claims to be no more—and no less!—than an ordinary
citizen whom God has laid hold of and who must therefore
speak. He shared in no human plot or political rebellion;
he spoke for God and his people. To expel the prophet was
therefore not simply getting rid of an undesirable alien, it
was to refuse to hear God's word, and so to be involved in
terrible and tragic consequences.

16 f. If God's warnings went unheeded, his judgments
would prove inescapable. Amos declared that the full
horrors of ancient war would engulf Israel the nation and
Amaziah the priest: women would be raped, all young men
and women slain, the property of the conquered shared
out among the victors (THY LAND SHALL BE DIVIDED BY
LINE) and the whole population deported as prisoners of

war. The survival of the prophecy in Israel's literature is
adequate comment on the story of Amaziah and Amos.

THE FOURTH EVENT-VISION: SUMMER FRUIT

8.1-3

If our guess be right, it was high summer when Amaziah
sent Amos back to Judah. We cannot say if Amos ever
returned; but we may well surmise that if God gave him a
further message, he would go back and deliver it. The
vision of the summer fruit belongs to the late summer, at
the time of the fruit harvest. As Amos looked one day at
a basket of summer fruit (called *qayiç* in Hebrew) he heard
the name repeated in his inward ear as *qeç*—'end'. It is
impossible to reproduce the prophetic pun in English,
though we can make a parallel one on the word 'basket'
if we translate it 'hamper'. To the voice, 'What do you
see, Amos?' he replied, 'A hamper of summer fruit.' The
voice continued, 'My people shall be hampered.' In this
illumination of a common autumn experience by a divine
insight Amos learns anew that Israel will come to its end
as a nation. Again he hears the divine voice say that there
will not be another 'pass-over' for Israel. This time doom
will come—ineluctable and final. Israel has broken the
covenant made with God; she cannot now avoid the
consequences.

The absence, in the fourth event-vision, of any pleading
for Israel suggests that it is in its proper place after Amos
had received from Amaziah such manifest tokens of the
rejection of his message.

IV

FURTHER SERMON MATERIAL

8.4–9.10

CALLOUSNESS AND CATASTROPHE

8.4-9

If the present arrangement of material in the book of Amos
has any historical significance, this section alone, coming as
it does after the visions of the year of the prophet's expul-
sion from Bethel, would indicate that he was not silenced
by the actions of Amaziah. The prophet returns to the
spiritual rottenness at the heart of commercial prosperity.
His words are reminiscent of the denunciation in 2.6-8,
though here he seems to be concerned with some traders'
guild which he deems largely responsible for the deteriora-
tion of commercial morality (cf. the use of 'we' for the
traders denounced). To MAKE THE POOR OF THE LAND TO
FAIL is literally to exterminate them. The avaricious
profiteers were impatient with the Sabbath and the great
religious holiday-festivals, because their shops had to be
shut and so no money could be made. Amos exposed their
shameful use of a double set of weights—the ephah, used
for making sales, was cut down, and the shekel by which
purchases were effected, was made heavier. These traders
would even deal in men and women, and sell rotten wheat.

Commercial morality could not become more callous or calculating.

Amos foresees the retribution coming as a (or the?) great earthquake (cf. 1.1), which he compares in its moving of the land to the rising and falling of the Nile flood waters, and also as being realized in an eclipse which will take sunlight from broad noon. We know an earthquake came; we also know that an eclipse, with its centre in Asia Minor, took place on 15 June, 763 BC. This suggests that Amos is still using natural catastrophes to serve as signs of the coming judgment of God. The first result of God's intervention would be utter national despair (vv. 9 f.). The present confident religiosity would be exposed for what it was, and the great religious FEASTS would become times of MOURNING, and the whole national life like a great funeral day.

THE FEARFUL FAMINE

8.10-14

Here Amos continues the use of natural calamities as signs of the coming retribution. He sees God's judgment on Israel as (and in all probability through) a famine. The prophet knows and pictures the distress of a land where there is neither bread to eat or water to drink, and he uses his knowledge to say that the anxious desire of a people that has by callousness lost its ability to hear and know the Word of God is even more tragic and distressing. Man does not live by bread alone! FROM SEA TO SEA originally meant 'from the Mediterranean Sea to the Dead Sea' (i.e. a famine confined to Israel herself), but later it meant from

the sea at one edge of the flat earth to that on the other
side of the world; and doubtless for Amos' later disciples
this prophecy was of an universal famine of God's Word.

14. This verse is difficult. It is clearly meant to denounce
the basic idolatry of Israel. If SIN OF SAMARIA be read, we
must understand it to refer to the sin of offering worship
and service to false gods. But in all probability the Revised
Standard Version is right to accept a slight emendation of
the Hebrew vowels and translate: THOSE WHO SWEAR BY
ASHIMAH OF SAMARIA, AND SAY, 'AS THY GOD LIVES. O DAN,'
where Ashimah is a god also referred to in II Kings 17.30
as worshipped at Hamath. THE MANNER OF BEERSHEBA is
similarly a reference to idolatrous ways of worship at Beer-
sheba, or even, if some scholars be right, in their slight
emendation of the text to make it conform to the LXX, a
direct reference to THY GOD, O BEERSHEBA. Such idolatry,
says Amos, is literally spiritual starvation diet! It cannot
end in anything but death.

INESCAPABLE DOOM

9.1-10

Amos' last vision of judgment and destruction begins, not
inappropriately for a prophet so sensitive to the reality of
worship, in the temple. We may reasonably suppose that
on his visit to Bethel after his encounter with Amaziah he
went once more into the royal temple, whose practices he
had exposed as grossly insincere. There he saw once again
the altar, and all the apparatus of worship that ought both
to establish and preserve good and peaceful relationships

between God and his people. But in Israel, because of her
false worship and her disobedient life, the house of God
could stand for nothing but inescapable doom. As Amos
looks at the temple, so grand and magnificent to his countryman's eye, he sees the fearful reality of the situation Israel
is in. He sees God standing at the altar and realizes he has
come for judgment. The language that follows is the language of the earthquake, and it may well be that Amos was
present when the great earthquake (cf. 1.1) struck Bethel,
and that he at once proclaimed its occurrence as the beginning of the judgment of God. Certainly that supposition
gives vivid meaning to these last verses of doom and threat.
As words uttered as the earthquake struck they recall all
that Amos has said is to happen besides, and make it plain
that, no matter where refuge be sought, the divine retribution will not let any escape.

The final word is that what happened in the temple as
the earthquake shook it, and what is going to happen in
the impending invasion, is not another 'natural calamity'
or another 'exploit of alien arms', but is fundamentally an
act of God. THE LORD GOD OF HOSTS IS HE THAT TOUCHETH
THE LAND; . . . HE HATH FOUNDED HIS TROOP IN THE
EARTH; . . . THE LORD IS HIS NAME. For sinful, careless, prosperous Israel it was to be A FEARFUL THING TO
FALL INTO THE HANDS OF THE LIVING GOD (Heb. 10.31).

But even in this moment of exultation when the prophet
sees what he believes to be the beginning of the fulfilment
of all that he has prophesied of doom and foreboding,
something else has to be said. It may be that some critics
are right who hold that the tenderer strain is due to the
influence of Amos' disciples, at any rate in its present
literary form. But the whole book of Amos is aware of the
fundamentally gracious and loving concern of God for his

people, and it is not therefore surprising that a reminder of the love that underlies even God's sternest judgments should be found here.

7. Here Amos has a final word to say to those who would argue that Israel must have specially favoured treatment from God, because of the unique relationship between Yahweh and Israel that had been established when God brought his people up out of Egypt. To these the prophet answers that God also placed the Ethiopians where they are, brought the Philistines from Caphtor (Crete) and the Syrians from Kir (in the distant north-east). That is to say, God's purpose for Israel is not the only purpose which he has in the world, and Israel is not of herself indispensable to God, any more than is Syria or Ethiopia or Philistia. God is more bound by the justice and righteousness of his own immutable nature than by a bond which a fickle Israel has sinfully broken again and again. So God is perfectly free to destroy the sinful kingdom of Israel, and announces his intention to do so. Only then can the exception be made: SAVING THAT I WILL NOT UTTERLY DESTROY THE HOUSE OF JACOB, SAITH THE LORD.

Amos is here getting as near to the NT categories of death and resurrection as his OT standing allows. He knows that THE WAGES OF SIN IS DEATH, and that doom he has announced to the nation. But he also knows that THE GIFT OF GOD IS ETERNAL LIFE, and he has done what he can to embody that in his message. We need not be surprised at a fumbling statement of the paradox, but rather wonder at the depth of the revelation which was given to Amos, and which, before the advent of Christ, he saw. His final statement can be taken as the perception of what he believed to be a necessary destruction. This evil generation must die, if in any way Israel is to survive: all those fundamentally irreligious people, who claim that, because of their religion, the calamities the prophet had foretold could not possibly come to pass, must perish. Until men could see further and deeper than that, there was no path forward to perfect life with God (v. 10).

V

EPILOGUE
EVENTUAL RESTORATION

9.11-15

It is commonly believed by scholars that these verses are a later addition to the book of Amos, and their belief is probably right. But it is most important to avoid the view that these verses are a merely sentimental 'happy ending' to enable an otherwise morose and unwanted prophecy to squeeze its way into the canon of Scripture. On the contrary, the verses themselves are designed to refer back to the previous text and recall the lessons it taught (see esp. vv. 14 f. which recall the prophecy of 5.11, and the use of MY PEOPLE OF ISRAEL after all that was said about Israel's end in 8.1-3). If anything the epilogue asserts, by its very presence at its particular place, that everything that Amos had said about God as the Lord of history, and about the moral and spiritual demands he made upon his people, was true. Later events had driven that home, and no future life of God's people could be blessed unless the divine demands were heeded. But, if God's requirements were fulfilled, then the future was unbelievably and unimaginably bright.

In that day became, for the later Hebrew writers, almost a technical term for referring to two great periods of God's activity—in the past, either at the Exodus from Egypt or at the height of David's success as conqueror of surrounding peoples; and in the future, when all the hopes engendered by both Exodus from Egypt and Davidic empire would be more than fulfilled in the historical realization of God's final purpose for the world. The meaning of v. 11 is, then, that when the day of God's final action comes, Israel will be completely restored. The prophecy anticipates the renewal of the Davidic empire (v. 12) in which Edom and other peoples were David's vassal states. But the prophecy is phrased so that it is clear that in the future, as in the past, the truth of the relationship between Israel and her subjects is not just that of conqueror to the conquered, but of both as belonging to God. For in conquest, past or future, it is THE LORD THAT DOETH THIS. Edom receives special mention not only because of its age-long and bitter repugnance to Israel (cf. Gen. 27; Num. 20.14-21) but because the realization of the new fraternal relationships would be a severer test of sincerity than with any other people.

In those days of new social, political and religious relationships, nature itself will develop a new and miraculous fertility. Crops will come so richly to harvest that it would take all the summer to gather them in; the ploughman would want to be on the fields before all the grain was gathered (v. 13). In effect, this would be a reversal of the sparse and famine conditions which Amos had foretold to his generation; but the basic theological insights are the same—a proper relationship to God is the only basis of proper relationships between his creatures, just as a proper relationship of each point of the circumference of a circle to the centre is the only basis of proper relationships between the points on the circumference.

The last two verses embody the final conviction that in the end God is a God of restoration, forgiveness and life,

not merely a God of destruction, retribution and death. God
will restore Israel, purged by the purifying fire of his
judgment, to all, and more than all, that she had had before.
To that bright prospect, of a people at one with their God,
there is no ending. THEY SHALL NO MORE BE PULLED UP OUT
OF THEIR LAND WHICH I HAVE GIVEN THEM, SAITH THE LORD
THY GOD. Once Israel had learnt that *all* she had—her
existence as a nation, her security as a power, the fertility
of her soil, the prosperity of her trade, the sanctity of her
religious rites and ceremonies—all derived from God and
were his gifts demanding obedient response, then all the
blessings of God's ideal Kingdom would be hers.

The lessons of Amos are not final. But he brings us as
far as any OT figure can—to the point where nothing but
the message of the Cross and Resurrection can meet our
question. For Amos, with unerring insight, long ago per-
ceived that the heart of the mystery of human life lay in
the balance of mercy and judgment in the heart of God.
If that mystery has been opened up with saving power to
Christian people in the message of the Cross and Resurrection of the Lord Jesus Christ, that does not make the book
of Amos irrelevant or outmoded. Rather does it point
across the centuries to the obedience which is due from
those who know themselves to be God's people to him
who has promised, and given, a full salvation in Jesus
Christ.

THE BOOK OF
MICAH

INTRODUCTION

THE REIGN OF HEZEKIAH 715-692

The opening verse of the book of Micah states that THE
WORD OF THE LORD CAME TO MICAH THE MORASHTITE[1] IN
THE DAYS OF JOTHAM, AHAZ, AND HEZEKIAH, KINGS OF JUDAH.
But in Jer. 26.18 we read that MICAH THE MORASHTITE
PROPHESIED IN THE DAYS OF HEZEKIAH KING OF JUDAH. The
two statements could both be true, but critics have recently
put forward urgent arguments for believing that none of
the prophetic oracles in our book of Micah really demand a
date in the reigns of Jotham or Ahaz. It is possible to suppose that even though we have no oracle from the earlier
prophecies of Micah the information in Micah 1.1 is correct,
though the earlier oracles have not been preserved. That
would give us the period from 750-692 as the maximum
possible period of prophetic activity—58 years, which is
not impossible but not highly probable. The minimum possible consistent with 1.1 would be from 736-692 or 42
years, again a long ministry for such a period. It is better
therefore, in view of the judgments made upon the relevance
of our book to the reign of Hezekiah, to suppose that the
present collection contains Micah's oracles delivered in that
reign, together with oracles preserved from the previous
period and made relevant anew in the time of Hezekiah.
and oracles uttered much later (as we shall see) which relate

---

[1] The RV spelling, not that of the AV, is correct here.

what Micah's disciples believed to be his true teaching to the circumstances of a later day.

But within the reign of Hezekiah it would seem fairly clear that Micah's activity is concerned with the approach of the Assyrian forces in 711 BC. He then prophesied for Jerusalem a fate like that of Samaria in 721, when the prophecy of Amos had been proved correct. But Jerusalem escaped destruction in 711 BC and Micah was somewhat discredited. But he came to full activity again in the crisis of 701 BC, when Sennacherib threatened to overrun all the land. Once more he prophesied destruction for Jerusalem, and once more he was to be found in error, though Jeremiah suggests that his word of doom had the effect on Hezekiah which Amos had hoped for in the northern kingdom but had not found: for Jeremiah says: DID NOT HE (HEZEKIAH) FEAR THE LORD, AND BESOUGHT THE LORD, AND THE LORD REPENTED HIM OF THE EVIL WHICH HE HAD PRONOUNCED AGAINST THEM? (Jer. 26.19). It would seem then that Micah prophesied in the reign of Hezekiah predominantly in connection with two great crises in Jerusalem and Judah; we may thus 'date' his ministry as lasting from about 712 to 700 BC.

What was Judaean life like in those days? Very much like that in the Israel that Amos knew and denounced. For Micah deals with the Judaean version of the development of a commercial and 'secular' culture. He attacks the same ruthless expropriation of the peasant farmer, the same dishonesty in the judges and the ruling classes, the same idolatry, sapping morale and destroying morality; the same debasement of the priesthood. At a time when Judah was living between two great powers—as Israel today lives between East and West—there was much political intrigue in high places. A pro-Egyptian party vied with a pro-Assyrian party for the ear of the king. We can read much more about that in the story of Isaiah of Jerusalem, Micah's great contemporary. And though for a while the king turned to the tasks of a religious reformation for national renewal, he was unable in the end to carry his activity through and to rescue his foreign policy from the expediency that made it weak and inconstant; and his successors undid what good he had done in the religious sphere. Though Micah's promise of doom for Jerusalem was not soon fulfilled, the city only staggered from crisis to crisis for one more century.

MICAH THE PROPHET

We know very little of Micah as a person. His name, like many in the OT shows that his parents were faithful Yahwists themselves, though, as we hear nothing of them, they may have been people of humble origin, or else the prophetic school (or Micah himself) has suppressed their names in order to leave what authority his word has clearly independent of such human commendation as having come from a noble family! He was a citizen of Moresheth-Gath (1.14), a small town in the foothills on the edge of the Philistine plain, a frontier post and outward defence point for Jerusalem up in the hills. By contrast with Amos' rather bare and desert countryside, Micah's home is in a fertile valley, where many yeomen farmers raised their crops generation after generation.

Micah had, like Amos, the simple heart of the countryman. He was not lured away by the glittering facade of the new culture—fine houses, advanced fashions, get-rich-quick businesses—but kept a firm grip on the moral realities that make for true national greatness. He shared Amos' passion for justice, and was particularly concerned with the same ruthless expropriation of peasant farmers as Amos had protested against in Israel. Like his previous namesake Micaiah-ben-Imlah (I Kings 22.14-28), he was not afraid to speak the unpopular word, and to speak it all alone.

Perhaps the worst difficulty facing Micah was that which also faced Micaiah—the popular and welcome belief that because Judah was God's people, their security could never be destroyed. IS NOT THE LORD AMONG US? NONE EVIL CAN COME UPON US (3.11). Micah's task, like that of Amos, was to teach an unwilling people that divine security was not to be divorced from moral obedience and sincere worship. The common view was that divine security could always be bought—with THOUSANDS OF RAMS, WITH TEN THOUSANDS OF RIVERS OF OIL (6.7). But he had to make it plain that God could not be corruptly bought like that. The only things that God required of his people were justice among themselves, charity as their prized guide, and a humble acceptance thereupon of what God's providence sent. That is the unassailable security of Yahweh's people.

Micah's word on behalf of the God who loved Judah, like that of Amos, had to be stern and foreboding. It seems that his word had some effect, for Jeremiah, about a century later, tells us that the reformation under Hezekiah was the product of Micah's ministry (Jer. 26.19). This is an important fact to remember when we read the accepted (and probably accurate) critical judgment that we have no prophecies stemming from Micah himself which speak of anything else but doom. But the fact that his disciples of later ages felt it right and fitting to include prophecies of hope alongside those of their master indicates, as I have observed in the commentary, that such oracles were not wholly foreign to Micah himself. Certainly we cannot imagine a spirit so sensitive to human suffering and misery being morosely dissatisfied if the doom he had rightly predicted was avoided by reformation.

Micah prophesied in Jerusalem, bringing to the attention of the nation's great capital city, with its big business men, its politicians, military leaders, priests and judges, the price in social morality that the nation was paying for its economic advance. He was not, like his contemporary Isaiah, profoundly concerned with the theology of politics; he was anxious to make the whole nation see that social crimes, though they may be covered up by the powers of transgressors to buy off any human judgment, could not and would not go unrewarded by God. And he made the great city culture aware of the social wickedness that was being done in the countryside. Yet basically his message is religious, not social; for he sees all life as a responsibility borne by man before God.

OUTLINE OF MICAH

I

THE CRISIS: THE ENEMY WITHOUT

1.1-16

II

THE ENEMIES WITHIN

2.1–3.12

Note: From Micah to his successors

III

TWO WAYS TO PEACE

4.1–5.15

IV

WHAT GOD REQUIRES

6.1-8

V

JUDGMENT AND HOPE

6.9–7.20

COMMENTARY ON MICAH

I

THE CRISIS: THE ENEMY WITHOUT
1.1-16

THE MAN WHO PROPHESIED

1.1

Like Amos, and every other great OT prophet, Micah speaks THE WORD OF THE LORD. It was his conviction, as it was that of Amos, that what *he saw* in vision and declared to his people was not his own 'bright idea', but a divine communication he could do no other than deliver (cf. Micah 3.8; Amos 7.15, etc.). As in the case of Amos, Micah's words are preserved to us not because he wrote them down and published them himself, but because for decades and centuries they were treasured by generations of devoted disciples, who continued to believe that what Micah said was the word of God (as we know many did in the days of Jeremiah), and preserved them for the treasury of Hebrew prophecy known as the Scroll of the Twelve.

Micah lived at Morasheth (or Mareshah), known today as Marissa. He was a 'borderer', citizen of a small country town, taken frequently on business to the capital cities of Samaria and Jerusalem, and, like Amos, profoundly distressed by what he saw in the big cities. Though his work here seems directed specially to two major crises in Judah's history (those of 711 and 701 BC), it clearly had a wider relevance. He was, as a later age acknowledged, largely responsible for Hezekiah's reforming policies, and the editor of his work evidently believed that what he said was related to nearly half a century of Judah's history (737 to 692 BC).

Like Amos, Micah ' saw ' his message, and we may suppose that there were both actual visions, and also that insight into events which also characterized Amos' work. At the start we are told that his messages concerned Samaria and Jerusalem. The life of the capital city certainly offers a fair indication of the quality of a nation's morale, but, more than that, in OT thinking the capital city stood for the whole nation, just as the king or the priest could embody the whole nation in other ways.

CAPITAL CRIMES AND THEIR PUNISHMENT

1.2-9

The opening section can be analysed into three parts. Vv. 2-4 are a psalm, or part of a psalm, which portrays, for the edification of all people (2 ab), with what awe-inspiring power God will come to visit his people. The critics who detect this as a product of a time later than Micah are probably right, though for the exegete it is important to remember that the use of such a later psalm is for two chief reasons : first, to make it plain that in Micah's own view, and in the tested experience of that view for many decades, what he had to say about Samaria and Jerusalem was of more than immediate and local significance; and, secondly, to emphasize in writing what would have been clear to Micah's hearers—that he was not ' selling his own opinions' but declaring revealed truth about the inevitable actions of God. Vv. 5 f., 8 f., constitute Micah's first message to Israel and Judah. Some scholars hold that since the address to Jerusalem is directed to the crisis of 711, the part of the prophecy concerning Samaria should be translated into the English present tense (as it is certainly permissible to do). But there is no great reason why we should do that, rather than suppose that Micah did address himself to Samaria's crisis some years before he first spoke to Jerusalem, and that the coalescence of the two prophecies occurred in the pre-literary or pre-canonical stage of the tradition. But either view is possible. V. 7 is almost certainly an addition to the tradition from post-exilic times, when idolatry was a much more consciously opposed transgression. Even so, two comments need to be made—first, that from Solomon's time onward there had been ' strange worship' in Jerusalem (cf. I Kings 11.1-8) and that Hezekiah, under the influence of Micah (Jer. 26.19), himself instituted a reformation which sought to abolish idolatry from Judah; and second, that such a post-exilic addition would serve to make it plain to a later generation that the actual message of the historic Micah was relevant and authoritative still.

2-4. The peoples of the earth are summoned to be witnesses of what happens when God comes down to earth from his heavenly temple: it will prick their consciences (BE WITNESS AGAINST). If there is anthropomorphism in the thought of God walking in the mountain tops, it is in transcendent form, for, where God walks, THE MOUNTAINS (the most solid, stable things the Hebrews knew) WILL BE MOLTEN, and they shall flow into the valleys, like wax melting before a fire or like water poured on to a steep slope. (THE VALLEYS SHALL BE CLEFT really makes no sense, and the word 'valleys' should be governed by a preposition, with a translation as above.) This is the background of the whole prophecy of Micah, and indeed, of all the prophets. Man does not live alone on the earth, with God remote, inaccessible, and unconcerned. Rather man lives his life in the sight and presence of God; and even if at times it seems that God is absent, the time will come when his presence and power will be revealed. The time of Micah's prophecy is such a time.

5, 6, 8, 9. God's visitation is imperative and, in the divine nature, unavoidable, because of the sins of Israel and Judah, epitomized for Micah in the life of Samaria and Jerusalem. Rather like Amos before him, Micah begins his address to Jerusalem by a denunciation that he had made previously against Samaria (5 ab, 6), and reminds his Judaean hearers, to the satisfaction of their irreligious complacency, that Samaria is now a rubbish heap, with its stones scattered and the foundations of its once proud buildings exposed, good for nothing but to provide the stones for a vineyard site on the hillside. In vv. 8 f. Micah proclaims his purpose to utter his prophecy in symbolic acts. He is to go about Jerusalem in the nude (i.e. unclothed in the technical sense, though with a labourer's loin-cloth on) to portray the barrenness that would soon come upon the city. The WAILING LIKE THE DRAGONS is another meaningless translation, which should be rendered 'jackals'. Similarly OWLS, though making sense, ought to be translated 'ostriches'. The picture we have is of Micah acting like a grief-stricken and utterly destitute mourner, trying to tell Jerusalem that his was but a picture of the destiny that would soon be hers.

9. Here we learn the reason. The sin of Israel and Samaria,
over which the Judaeans gloated as the cause of her destruction, had poisonously infected Jerusalem and Judah. The
infection was not slight and momentary, but HER WOUND
WAS INCURABLE. The sins of Israel had COME UNTO JUDAH,
even to the very centre, TO JERUSALEM. And just as every
city had its gate, where justice was publicly administered,
so Jerusalem was the 'gate' of Judah. Now that Israel's sin
was there, it would have to be dealt with.

7. The perennial root of Samaria's and Jerusalem's sin
was idolatry. The verse itself comes from the post-exilic
period when the returned Jews despised the image worship
of the Samaritans. At either time, the Scripture wants to say,
the sins of others are also your own! THE HIRES in the
earlier part of the verse refers to the presents brought for
the image-deities, to buy their favours; in the latter part
HIRE probably means the payment made for 'sacred
prostitution'. Micah and his later disciples knew that there
was no good, no godliness, and no future in any such forms
of worship.

'CRY HAVOC'

1.10-16

This material, vivid and, it must be confessed, somewhat
enigmatic, seems to be connected with the Assyrian crisis
of 711 BC. By its juxtaposition to vv. 2-9 we may assume
that when the crisis came and the advance of Assyria was
known, Micah was in Jerusalem, actually engaged upon
his 'wailing mission'. A recent commentator (Rolland E.

Wolfe in *The Interpreter's Bible*) has surmised that when he received the news Micah went on a ' Paul Revere's ride ' back to his home town of Mareshah, passing through the various places named in this section. But this, even with rearrangement to provide a more rational itinerary, would hardly be a possible route, and the supposition that Micah went on a mission of information hardly coincides with the opening lines of the poem. It is more likely, therefore, that what we have here is Micah's reaction to the news about the Assyrian advance, and to information received in Jerusalem about the reaction of some of the border towns of the south-west to a request for aid.

Interpretation is rendered more difficult, because in the poem each place name is made the basis of a pun, which has sometimes been ' explained ' by later scribes, to the confusion of both text and meaning for us. It is hardly possible for us to produce the plays on words in an English translation, though ' They pressed on at Preston ' would be a fair modern equivalent. The sum of the whole section is that there can be no possible escape from complete defeat by the Assyrian armies. Never perhaps, had a prophet so impressive a response in events as wailing Micah in Jerusalem.

10. Declare ye it not at Gath. These are the opening words of David's lament over Saul and Jonathan. David had counselled keeping the news of the extent of Hebrew losses from the Philistines at Gath, lest they should be encouraged to follow up their victory, and win even more significant battles against defeated Israel. Micah evidently believed the Assyrian advance to be as threatening to Judah now as the unexploited position of the Philistines was then, but that fact must, for prudence' sake, be kept secret.

In the house of Aphrah (better: In Beth-le-Aphrah) **roll thyself in the dust.** Here the name Aphrah is a pun on the Hebrew word for dust; and to roll in the dust was a manifestation of grief and mourning (cf. Jer. 6.26; Ezek. 27.30).

11. Pass ye away, thou inhabitant of Saphir. This verse continues the punning prophecy in a prediction of these townsmen marching away as prisoners of war, when, stripped of their garments, they would have their SHAME NAKED. The rest of the verse offers difficulties of text and interpretation. That THE INHABITANTS OF ZAANAN CAME NOT FORTH may be a report upon the failure of Zaanan to send any men for the defence force at Jerusalem, and so add to the certainty of defeat for both places. The rest of the verse is better retranslated to read: 'Beth-ezel is removed from its site', i.e., is razed to the ground.

12. The population of Maroth evidently could not believe the bad news. Surely God would not let his people be conquered and his land overrun! So they WAITED CARE-FULLY (anxiously) FOR GOOD news, which never came. On the contrary evil, i.e. calamity, came from God to the very gate of Jerusalem.

13. Lachish was a town only some four miles from Micah's home. Doubtless there was much talk of the establishment at Lachish of a 'chariot brigade' involving the introduction of the horse, the 'new weapon' of great mobility and power. The advent of the horse was criticized much by the prophets, for not only did it of itself tend to create feelings of self-sufficiency in the men who used them, who thought that military victory could be obtained by sufficiently strong chariot formations, but also, since horses came from Egypt (or other foreign power), there were inevitable religious compromises associated with whatever alliance was necessary to obtain the horses desired, much as in the modern world Russia will sell or lend arms only on certain political conditions. Apparently Lachish was the first 'chariot station', and so was THE BEGINNING OF SIN to Jerusalem (THE DAUGHTER OF ZION) for whose defence the chariot brigade existed. In doing this Judah was but following the bad example of Israel (13c).

14. The present given to Moresheth-Gath is the dowry which a father gives to his daughter when she is joined to another family. Moresheth-Gath is to be handed over to another owner, and an indemnity paid as well. Achzib means 'winter brook', i.e. a stream that dries up during the summer when water is most needed. Achzib will be like that to the king, declining aid when it is most needed. Hence the use of the word LIE.

15. An heir. Really the conqueror, who will receive Moresheth as his own. The situation will repeat the time when David was in hiding in the cave of Adullam. The vaunted glory of Israel will be found in hiding again.

16. Shaving the head was a sign of mourning, though forbidden by Deuteronomy (14.1). EAGLE should be 'vulture' which has a bald neck. Judah must mourn because her children will be lost to her in captivity as prisoners of war.

II

THE ENEMIES WITHIN

2.1–3.12

To the great prophets of the OT no crisis was purely military or political. It is a likely conjecture that, in the days immediately before the news of the Assyrian advance reached Jerusalem, wailing Micah, having drawn the attention of the citizens by his dramatic behaviour, took advantage of their presence to drive home the lessons found in this section, where the life of Judah is exposed for what it is. The verses embody the country dweller's protest against the unjust expropriation of peasant farmers, the false sense of security engendered by a callous prosperity, and the irreligion that could prefer pleasant untruths from manifestly hireling prophets to the cleansing, demanding, difficult word of the living God.

EXPOSURE OR EXPLOITATION

2.1-10

Micah now reveals how the social and economic evils which characterized the Israel to which Amos spoke are now found in Judah. Amos had inveighed against those who could not wait for Sabbath or feast day to pass so that they might indulge their dishonest trade (Amos 8.5); Micah now attacks those who cannot tolerate night for rest, but use it to plan more evil schemes. As soon as day dawns the plans begotten in darkness are put into effect, with no thought of whether they are right or wrong, pleasing or displeasing to God, but only the reflection that ' I can get away with it; why not? '. The evils Micah is concerned with are those of wealthy traders and rich landlords who buy up real estate by economic pressure, seizure and distraint of land and houses, and, if necessary, by actual violence.

2. A man and his house means a man and his family and all his servants, i.e. all the living members of a peasant household running a farm.

A man and his heritage means the property seen, for what it was esteemed, as a sacred trust to be handed on from father to son. This evil process of expropriation prevented any inheritance being passed on.

3. Here Micah turns the tables against the exploiters, who, he says, will receive at God's hands the measure they have meted out.

Against this family means against the landlords and exploiters regarded as a group or class in the nation. AN EVIL means, of course, a calamity or misfortune. The wealthy exploiters would soon find themselves yoked together as slaves and prisoners of war, and it would be a yoke from which there could be no escape. (Perhaps there were some special ' safety yokes ' available for those who used oxen for work.) When that day came the wealthy would no

longer walk proudly or HAUGHTILY. It would be an EVIL
TIME for them.

4. This verse becomes intelligible once it is realized that
the preposition AGAINST should be translated 'on behalf
of'. Micah is saying that when the evil blow falls one of the
deported will sing a lamentation for them all. HE HATH
CHANGED THE PORTION means changed the 'lot' or
'property'; HOW HE HATH REMOVED IT FROM ME means
'how is it that God could take our property away from
us!' In this saying Micah might well be using familiar and
conventional cries of the tenants the wealthy had evicted.
It would seem that God had forsaken them and divided
their fields among the alien conquerors.

5. This thought is carried home—the wealthy will have no
one left in THE CONGREGATION (or assembly—the Hebrew
word is as near 'church' as we can get in OT Hebrew) OF
THE LORD—the exploiters of the poor would not only be
exiled from home, but cut off from God and his people.
To CAST A CORD BY LOT is the means used to parcel out land;
the exiles will have no part in the sharing out of the inheritance of God's people. What they have done to the
poor in the economic sphere, God will do to them in the
religious one.

6. This verse is difficult. It represents some quick-fire re-
partee from Micah to some who interrupted his vehement
denunciations. They said to him, PROPHESY YE NOT, i.e.
'Don't say such things as you are saying.' Micah replied
(we can neglect the words in italics, for their being printed
so is a sign that they are not in the Hebrew, but are thought
necessary to make sense by the translators): PROPHESY,

i.e., a true prophet does not obey the commands of his audience, but of God. Again the hecklers shouted out, THEY SHALL NOT PROPHESY TO THEM! i.e. 'You must not talk like this to such wealthy, influential people!' Micah replied: THEY SHALL NOT TAKE SHAME, i.e., accepting the translation as it stands, *either* 'No true prophet can take notice of you, for he is the willing servant of his conscience, which he will not cause to shame him', *or* 'The hides of these exploiters are so thick that nothing that is said will ever make their consciences to accuse them!' A better translation, 'There must be no holding back of reproaches,' favours the former interpretation.

7. Micah then asks three questions of his audience, which is called (the implications is that though it has the name it may not possess the reality!) THE HOUSE OF JACOB: (1) IS THE SPIRIT OF THE LORD STRAITENED? i.e., Has God lost some of his power that you can so comfortably believe that he will not do as I say? (2) ARE THESE HIS DOINGS? i.e., Can people imagine that God approves the vicious use of economic power by the wealthy, as if the acts were his own? (3) DO NOT MY WORDS DO GOOD TO HIM THAT WALKETH UPRIGHTLY? i.e., the interrupters object only because Micah's words have stabbed their consciences awake. If they had been practising the justice and mercy God required (cf. 6.8) the same words, though minatory, would have come as a breath of fresh air, bringing the hope that, even at great cost, the evil and injustice would be purged away.

8 f. Micah continues his cataloguing of the crimes of the exploiters. Their action has had the same effect as if some enemy had come and evicted the Judaean peasant farmers from their properties, though this action was done by those

who were, and claimed to be, God's people! Things had
even got to the pitch that ordinary citizens going about their
ordinary peace-time avocations (AS MEN AVERSE FROM WAR)
were attacked by gangs of thugs, probably hired by some
wealthy ' quick-money' gangster, and stripped of clothes
and valuables alike. Nor have any chivalrous feelings for
women or children kept the same exploiters from turning
widows and orphans into the streets, homeless and outcast,
leaving Judah deprived of her posterity.

10. These Jerusalem addresses of wailing Micah conclude
with an order put into the mouth of the invading conqueror:
' ARISE, DEPART'. Those would be the words the exploiters
would have to obey when the tragedy came. THIS IS NOT
YOUR REST means ' not your inheritance', ' there is nothing
left for you here! ' The evil deeds of evil men had polluted
the whole land, and nothing short of destruction could
match the crime or heal the wound. THE WAGES OF SIN IS
DEATH.

THE POPULAR PROPHET

2.11

Micah had already found that he was an unpopular
prophet. Like Micaiah-ben Imlah's before him, his was the
one unwanted voice among many popular ones. Here Micah
shows to what irreligious extremities the evil condition of
of a people with a bad conscience could go. If they heard
a prophet who could tell them comfortable and deceptive
lies or said that he would prophesy to them for the mere
provision of wine and strong drink to stimulate him into

prophetic activity (OF WINE AND OF STRONG DRINK should be
translated ' for ') then they would take him as their prophet,
and Micah the true prophet would remain unheeded.

GOD'S GOODNESS BEYOND TRAGEDY

2.12 f.

If this is, as the critics seem rightly to argue, an inter-
polation dating from the late exile, it is more than a mere
balancing of Micah's doom by a later optimist. It is the
assertion by a later disciple who believed in a restoration
that Micah's judgment still remained true, even if it were
not the whole truth. If there is a gift of new life to be given
to men or to nations by God, there is no obliteration in that
gift of the fact that the wages of sin is death. As with Amos
and his disciples, so with Micah and his, there, is both at
the beginning of the tradition and more explicitly later on,
a conviction that the final answer to the deep mystery of
human iniquity must contain the assertion both of death
and resurrection. The final conditions for sharing this conviction clearly were not available until Christ had died and
risen from the dead, but we should do less than justice to
Amos and Micah if we did not see some anticipation of the
Christian doctrine here.

In v. 12 Micah is made to use the word ' remnant' which
had been coined by his elder contemporary Isaiah. God
promises to bring his scattered people together, like a shepherd gathering his flock together. BOZRAH was famed for its
well nourished sheep. The ' sheep' of the restored Israel
will be in THEIR FOLD—i.e., in a new Jerusalem; and, like
a large sheepfold noisy with many sheep, the restored city

will be humming with the activity of its large population.

13. The breaker is the ram who, by pushing with his strong horns, makes a way through the scrub for the flock.

They have broken up is *either* the fact that the waiting flock, once the breaker has found a way for them, is broken up as sheep follows sheep through the gap, *or* a mistranslation for 'broken through': the meaning is the same in either case.

The gate is the gate of Babylon, through which the exiles are to pass. THE BREAKER at the beginning of the verse, and the KING at the end are, of course, both metaphors for God. The work of restoration and recovery will be his.

CORRUPTION IN HIGH PLACES

3.1-4

This prophecy is addressed by Micah to both civic and national leaders. The occasion we do not know, but we may not unreasonably suppose that Micah made or was given an opportunity to speak to some deliberative gathering of leaders called in the light of the Assyrian emergency.

Heads of Jacob are the leaders of Jerusalem society.

Princes of the house of Israel are those responsible for government, and Micah reminds both parties that they are responsible for seeing that judgment (=justice) is maintained in its full integrity. Again Micah echoes Amos' words to Israel only a few years earlier, and again his plea is unheeded. Micah accuses the Judaean leaders of being the opposite of what they should be, for they HATE THE GOOD, AND LOVE THE EVIL. For this Micah regards them as treating the poor litigants as a butcher treats a slaughtered beast— tearing the skin from the flesh, and the flesh from the bones, reducing a living creature to three separate saleable commodities, just as the expropriators reduced a living homestead to three saleable commodities—land, house, and people to sell into slavery. In v. 3 Micah goes even further and likens the exploiters to men who not only reduce a living creature to commodities, but also devour it for the satisfaction of their own greed. The processes of expropriation are like chopping a beast up small for the cooking pot.

But, adds Micah, the day is at hand when these same men will cry to the Lord for mercy, as their victims have cried for mercy. But God will not answer; rather will he 'hide' himself from them because their evil conduct has deserved retribution. The wages of sin must be paid.

THE FALSE PROPHETS AND THE TRUE

3.5-8

This is another theme in which Micah is like both Amos and Micaiah. There were plenty of prophets to utter comforting though deceiving messages—if the hearers paid their fees! These men were professional prophets, obtaining their living from their 'calling'. The dangers inherent in the situation are manifest, and Micah makes it plain that, as a class, the professional prophets of his day had become entirely unprincipled and mercenary.

The false prophets are said to BITE WITH THEIR TEETH,
AND CRY ' PEACE '. This means that if they receive for their
prophesyings a fee sufficient to maintain their standard of
living, they are quite ready to tell their clients what they
want to hear. Instead of joining Micah in pointing out the
moral and spiritual realities behind the Assyrian crisis,
they merely said : ' Peace '—' There won't be any war. Don't
worry at all! ' On the other hand if any client PUTTETH NOT
INTO THEIR MOUTHS, i.e., does not pay them a sufficiently fat
fee, they PREPARE WAR AGAINST HIM, i.e., make things hot
and uncomfortable. This they are able to do, because of their
professional monopoly; but their sense of security is
deceptive.

6. The real result of their prostitution of a divine office
and function is that they live in a world where there is
darkness so great that no visions can be seen. So the false
prophets are no longer able to descry the future, or speak a
word of God, for the true light of every true prophet has
been withdrawn from them. Their professional prostitution
has produced this impotence, though it is at the same time a
judgment of God. So THE SEERS WILL BE ASHAMED, because
they cannot see, THE DIVINERS CONFOUNDED (i.e. reduced to
silence by their inability to discern); all the false prophets
will COVER THEIR LIPS (either with the hand to indicate they
have nothing to say, or with their beard, to hide the whole
face for shame), and the basic reason for it all is that there
is NO ANSWER (i.e. no communication) OF GOD to them.

8. By contrast Micah speaks of his own certainty of hearing
and speaking God's word, and of his proper God-given
authority to do so. He is FULL OF POWER BY THE SPIRIT OF
THE LORD, and he has JUDGMENT (discernment or insight),

and the MIGHT which such divine endowments bring, and
it is by this divine power that he knows he is authorized
to expose the sins of his people. God has spoken to him,
we may say in Amos' words, and he can but prophesy.

THE NEMESIS OF CORRUPT
LEADERSHIP

3.9-12

Perhaps Micah had been asked after or during his address
to the nation's leaders for the authority by which he spoke
such uncomfortable words. He gave his answer by the contrast of the false prophet and the true in vv. 5-8; he now
resumes his denunciation, and does not mince his words.

9. He charges the leaders with being so perverted as to
have come to ABHOR JUDGMENT (here=justice), and to PER-
VERT ALL EQUITY. There was no fair dealing left in them.
They had indeed made a ' new Jerusalem ' out of the old,
but it was a Jerusalem (or Zion) built on violence and crime.

11. Micah makes the specific accusations that those who
administer justice give their verdicts for money received,
that the priests adapt their teaching to the desires of their
wealthiest clients, and that the prophets will give whatever
advice is wanted, provided they are paid for it. And all the
time—and this makes the crimes particularly heinous—they
pretend to serve and trust God, and think that, regardless
of their evil practices, God remains with them and will
allow no calamity to touch them. It is this irreligious confidence which causes the people to reject the witness of

Micah, and will lead, inevitably to the destruction of Jerusalem.

12. FOR YOUR SAKE, Micah says to the leaders, ZION SHALL BE AS A PLOWED FIELD, i.e. your false confidence is the reason for the nation's unwillingness to be prepared against difficulty, and for the enemy's belief that conquest will be easy. HEAPS are heaps of ruins, and the final word of Micah is that the MOUNTAIN OF THE HOUSE, i.e., the mountain (Zion) where the house of God was built, will be an uninhabited hilltop in the middle of a forest.

NOTE: FROM MICAH TO HIS SUCCESSORS

Micah's prophecy did not immediately come true. Neither in 711 nor in 701 was Jerusalem destroyed. By the standards of true prophecy preserved in Deut. 18.22 (WHEN A PROPHET SPEAKETH IN THE NAME OF THE LORD, IF THE THING FOLLOW NOT, NOR COME TO PASS, THAT IS THE THING WHICH THE LORD HATH NOT SPOKEN, BUT THE PROPHET HATH SPOKEN IT PRESUMPTUOUSLY) Micah was thus a false prophet, and would be disregarded. The fact that, nevertheless, his prophecies about the fall of Jerusalem were preserved shows that he and his disciples believed, in spite of all appearances to the contrary, that he had been charged with a true word from God. When Jerusalem fell, and the Judaeans were taken into captivity, then his disciples would naturally think that what he had said had come true. His works could be allowed circulation again. But we have the prophecies of the Assyrian crises together with exilic and post-exilic material. It would therefore seem that as the Jews returned to Jerusalem they brought even the sternest messages of Micah with them as making a permanently relevant comment on the life of God's people in the world. The returning exiles were buoyed up with great hopes, but they did not, apparently, wish to forget the intense moral realism of a prophet like Micah. His words stood—and stand—as a valid message for the people of God.

But the fact that Micah's disciples of a later period joined his prophecies with the more hopeful material coming from their circle in a later day, means that they would not have supposed that Micah's own message was entirely without hope. The further additions made in the post-exilic period, with their apparent reliance on armed power, show that the school which preserved the traditions of Micah were as divided as the rest of the nation about the way in which Judaism was to come to its ultimate destiny. Once more, we must be ready to see the naturalness of such tensions of theological and political judgment in a time before the Cross and Resurrection had revealed to all mankind what the way of the Messiah was, and by what path of death and resurrection the eternal Kingdom of God would be established.

As we leave ch. 3. we pass from the work of the historic, the 'wailing' Micah to the material that later inheritors of his tradition thought would both preserve the true spirit of their master, and show to a later generation the abiding relevance of his message.

III

TWO WAYS TO PEACE

4.1–5.15

In this section we have two strands of later material. Some comes from approximately the time of the second Isaiah, when the faithful Jews, the first ' Zionists', were looking forward to a return to Palestine. At this time Micah's disciples, like their contemporaries, looked to some miraculous inauguration of a new age. The other comes from a date in the post-exilic period when the Jewish State began to look forward to attaining her great dreams for the future under the guidance of a great military-religious leader. The two views scarcely harmonize, but they reflect the puzzles of the modern as well as of the ancient world.

PEACE BY MIRACLE

4.1-8

This section (v. 5 apart) is from the exilic strand in chapters 4 and 5. Part of it (vv. 1-3) appears also as an insertion in the prophecy of Isaiah (cf. Isa. 2.2-4). It looks forward to a future of universal peace issuing from a universal acknowledgement of the Lordship of Yahweh. The way in which the vision is presented indicates that the future contemplated will be the work of God—the whole earth will be reduced to a plain, and Mount Zion elevated to a point where she is everywhere visible. It is profitless speculation to wonder whether the writer and his readers really thought that the natural world would be thus physically changed, for whether they thought the language metaphorical or realistic, the purpose of making the statement was to indicate that, by some change impossible of achievement save by God, the radically new age would be wholly of God's making. Universal peace would come by a miracle.

In the last days referred originally to the last days of the Exile. Great hopes for the future of Jews and Gentiles alike were entertained by the zealous Zionists of the time, as can be seen from the work of Second Isaiah (cf. Isa. 40.4; 41.18-20; 44.5; 45.1-6, 14; 49.6-8, 22 f.). Zion is to be exalted, and many nations will go to there to worship the God of Israel.

2. God of Jacob means God of the people who claim to be Jacob's descendants = God of the Jews.

In that miraculous time when universal allegiance to Yahweh is realized, God will be judge among the nations. There will, of course, then be a commonly accepted standard of right and wrong. It will not be necessary to settle disputes by force, making might right: on the contrary, because a common right will be acknowledged (the ways of the Lord and his laws), there will be universal disarmament. The 'iron and steel industry' will be used for peaceful purposes only! There will be no more need for the arts of war. This will bring an age of prosperity and security: everyone will have his 'acre and a cow'—HIS VINE AND HIS FIG TREE— and possess them in security. (It was by an allusive use of this passage that, according to John, Jesus conveyed to Nathaniel that the wonderful new age of the world had begun in his appearing—cf. John 1.45-51.) The disciples of Micah, who knew something of long-unfulfilled prophecy, said, even of this far-off vision, THE MOUTH OF THE LORD HATH SPOKEN IT, i.e., it will certainly, sooner or later, come true.

5. This verse seems to breathe a different spirit, and some would claim it as a 'particularist' interjection into a universalist section. It may indeed express the views of one unfortunately irrepressible part of post-exilic Judaism, that which thought itself the sole possessor of the true religion, and the Gentiles not as future sharers in it, but as permanently given to the worship of false gods. Certainly the battle between 'particularists' and 'universalists' raged fiercely in post-exilic times, and the conflict is reflected in the OT by the books of Ruth, Jonah and Second Isaiah for the universalists, and by Ezra and Nehemiah for the particularists. The debate was not finished in Jesus' day, and he spoke and acted vigorously for the universalists, particularly when he 'cleansed the Temple' with the words: IS IT NOT WRITTEN, MY HOUSE SHALL BE CALLED OF ALL NATIONS THE HOUSE OF PRAYER? BUT YE HAVE MADE IT A DEN OF THIEVES (Mark 11.17). But it is equally, if not more, likely that this verse represents the attitude of the inheritors of the exilic prophecy of vv. 1-4, who found the wonderful but sanguine hopes unfulfilled in post-exilic days. The non-fulfilment of the prophecy (which THE MOUTH OF THE LORD had spoken) was not to be made an excuse for cynicism, despair, or the abandonment of Israel's religion. On the contrary, even though the Gentiles still seek other gods, we, the heirs of the one true faith, must remain for ever, whatever appear-

ances may suggest, loyal and obedient to our God. That is
how the faithful disciples of Micah's school might well have
intended this verse.

This interpretation is probably fortified by the fact that,
though it follows an unfulfilled prophecy, it precedes one
that was at least partially fulfilled. There was a new
beginning to Israel's life in Palestine, and even if the
theocracy dreamed of (THE LORD SHALL REIGN OVER THEM)
was not actualized, there was a substantial enough realization of the hopes of vv. 6 and 7 to give some expectation
that the fulness of the prophet's vision would be brought to
pass.

6. In that day refers, as does v. 1, to the time at the end of
the exile when God will ordain another 'Exodus' for his
people.

Her that halteth means wounded and limping Israel.

her that is driven out is the exiled people of Judah.

7. the Lord shall reign over them in mount Zion is an apt
addition in Micah's prophecy, where the lack of recognition
of God's authority had been so sharply stated.

8. Here we have a final picture of Judah in the new post-
exilic world, as the exilic disciples of Micah conceived it.
Zion (=Jerusalem) would, in contrast to the Jerusalem of
Micah's day, be the shepherd's watch tower, from which the
divine Shepherd would be able to watch and guard his flock.
(see II Kings 18.8 for a reference to the existence of such
towers).

daughter of Zion is a poetic Hebraism for Zion.

the first dominion is promised to Jerusalem, i.e. it will once
more be the capital of the largest empire Israel had known
—its first, under David and Solomon. In the setting of the
whole prophecy from vv. 1-8, this verse is surely meant as
an understatement, and the empire thought of as coming to
Jerusalem IN THAT DAY would be the whole of the known
and habitable world.

THROUGH TRAGEDY TO TRIUMPH

4.9-13

This section reflects the outlook of the circle of Micah's
disciples in the years when the returned exiles began to
realize that the opposition of other peoples to their resettle-
ment in Palestine was so violent and persistent (e.g. under
Zerubbabel in 516 BC and Menahem in 485 BC) that, unless
they resorted to arms themselves, their hopes of a home in
Palestine would never be realized.

To comfort themselves and their contemporaries, they re-
issued from their treasury a prophecy which had been first
uttered at the time of the collapse of the monarchy, when
Zedekiah fled and left the nation without a king. At that
time, apparently, a prophet in the circle had foreseen the
inevitability of the captivity in Babylon, but had also expressed his conviction, gained by divine inspiration, that
beyond the bitterness of exile God would once more raise
up his people (vv. 9 f.).

Why dost thou cry aloud? refers to the despair and wailing
of the days before the fall of Jerusalem.

Is there no king? . . . Is thy counsellor perished? refers to
the departure of Zedekiah, and is meant to remind the
people that the real ruler of Israel and her real counsellor,
God, had not left and would not leave her. Yet the people
behaved as if they were really in serious plight! God's
answer, through Micah's later disciple, was to say 'Be in
a serious plight, for so you are! You shall go out of Zion's
city into the open country, and from Palestine to Babylon.
Not till then will deliverance come. There the Lord will
redeem you from your enemies! '

We saw in studying Amos how close to the Christian con-
cept of death and resurrection he came. Here a disciple of
Micah at the time of the fall of Jerusalem, came very close
indeed to this same fundamentally Christian insight. The
nation would be restored, delivered, and brought back—but
only from the other side of defeat, destruction, national
' death '. Once more an OT prophet saw not only that THE
WAGES OF SIN IS DEATH but also that THE GIFT OF GOD IS
LIFE.

11-13. We come now to the contemporary post-exilic part
of this unit of prophecy. It portrays the general situation
with which the returned exiles had to contend for many
years. MANY NATIONS ARE GATHERED AGAINST THEE. They say,
LET HER BE DEFILED, i.e., let the new rebuilt city and temple
be pillaged and profaned again; and LET OUR EYE LOOK
UPON ZION, i.e., let us see what we can make of Zion.

Such were the evil intentions of hostile peoples. But they
reckoned without God, who is able to deal with nations as
easily as a farmer can bring his sheaves to the threshing
floor (v. 12). This means that instead of the nations coming
to wreak their spite on Zion, actually God will be bringing
them to a threshing floor where they will be threshed.

13. The thresher is named : ARISE AND THRESH, O DAUGHTER
OF ZION. Here some prophetic successor to Micah saw that
the Jews would have to take up arms, and he avows his
belief that even there God would aid his people miraculously. Israel would be the bull used for threshing. Her
horns would be IRON—and she would attack the nations
with them (iron = weapons of war); her HOOFS would be
BRASS—and she would trample the nations underfoot; many
nations would be beaten to pieces, i.e., would lose their
political identity in war with Israel.

The picture is of fierce battle, and of triumphant issue.
But, in the prophet's mind, the restored people of God who
resorted to arms would not suppose that their own strength
had won them victory, and therefore that they had a
right to all the spoils of war. On the contrary the assertion
that I WILL CONSECRATE THEIR GAIN UNTO THE LORD, AND
THEIR SUBSTANCE UNTO THE LORD OF THE WHOLE EARTH
means that God would be acknowledged as the true victor,
and, for that very reason, must receive all the prizes of war.
Even if Israel is to fight, she will fight only this holy war,
which, from beginning to end, declares the prophet, she
must see as a war for God.

THE WARRIOR KING

5.1-6

This section, also originating in post-exilic times, uses the
same device as 4.9-13, beginning its message by a reference
to the previous history of Judah, indeed going back beyond
the historic Micah to David's time, and then coming for-

ward to the contemporary situation with a message of
encouragement reinforced from the past.

1. This verse subtly reproduces the situation when the
Assyrians attacked Judah in Hezekiah's reign, and the army
had to be mobilized. The call to mobilization (GATHER
THYSELF IN TROOPS—or battalions) was as necessary in the
particular post-exilic period as then. Jerusalem, now being
rebuilt, was, as then, beseiged. THE JUDGES, as the last
representatives of civil government (for there was no king
when Zedekiah fled), were to be smitten WITH A ROD UPON
THE CHEEK, i.e., they were to be dispossesed of authority
and society would lose its last elements of civil structure.
Universal chaos would ensue.

In the second verse the compiler makes a bold leap
across the centuries back to the chaos that followed the
death of Saul and Jonathan, when David had to establish
his authority by what was, in effect, a protracted civil war.
Yet it was from the little and insignificant village Bethle-
hem-Ephratah that God brought forth the greatest of
Hebrew kings. The compiler-prophet means the post-exilic
Judaeans to believe that out of their contemporary chaos
God would similarly raise up a new and great king.

2. Ephratah is the name of the district round Bethlehem,
cited to distinguish it from other places with the same name.

the thousands of Judah are the villages (population, roughly
1,000), a governmental and civic unit, like the ' hundred ' in
England in the Middle Ages.

unto me, i.e., to God: the ruler was not to be, as Saul turned
out to be, a self-seeking monarch, but one devoted to the
will of God in all things.

whose goings forth have been from of old, from everlasting.
This means to say that the advent of the new ruler, wholly
given to God's will, will not be something newly conceived
by God, but the fulfilment of something that began as far
back as the monarchy began. EVERLASTING hardly conveys
the real sense of the Hebrew word, which is better rendered 'from ancient times'—a long, unspecified period.

This verse was used by Matthew in his story of the Wise
Men. It was there quoted by the priests and scribes in
answer to Herod's question about where they expected the
Messiah to be born—an evident sign to Jews as well as
Christians that the real RULER who should COME FORTH to
God would be born in Bethlehem. Matthew has often been
criticized for utilizing a prophecy taken from a passage
connected with so warlike a figure as is described in Micah
5.1-6. But that is not the only possible comment to make.
At the beginning of his Gospel Matthew is trying to indicate
the nature and function of its central figure as the one in
whom the life of the New Israel of God is to have its beginning and its eternal perfection and fulness. He writes a
genealogy of Jesus Christ to leave it plain that at the very
point where Jesus appears there was a break in the process
of human paternal begetting, and, by the convention of the
use of the passive voice (OF WHOM WAS BORN JESUS) there
was an act of God (Matt. 1.16). Here, in Matt. 2.5 f., the
same evangelist is trying to say that if the Jews are looking
for the figure of the great king who was to serve God and be
born in Bethlehem, they could find him in the figure and
person of Jesus. As for the plain fact that Jesus was not a
warrior-king, two things must be said. First, Matthew was
surely at least as much aware of that contrast as any of his
modern critics: what he was trying to do, in adapting such
a plainly difficult text to Christian use, was to claim that

all that the Jews of post-exilic and of Christian times looked
for in their own expectation of a warrior-Messiah was fulfilled, surpassed and transcended in the person and work
of Jesus Christ. Secondly, Matthew, like all the Evangelists,
knew that Jesus was a warrior, and captain of a host of
warriors. But his enemy was the devil, and his kingdom,
as John put it (John 18.36), NOT OF THIS WORLD. It was to
be fought for, but not as the world understood 'fighting'.
The use of the prophecy by Matthew and the Church is
thus illuminating, if we are willing to see text and reality
in the light of the category of a fulfilment that involves
transcendence rather than mere literalism.

3. Here the post-exilic compiler takes his thought and his
prophecy down to the time of the fall of Jerusalem, and
makes it plain that his view is that it was an event foreseen and foretold by the prophets, both as disaster and as
the prelude to a better restoration. When SHE WHICH
TRAVAILETH (Judah in captivity bringing into existence a
number who believed in a divinely ordained return) HATH
BROUGHT FORTH (a sufficient number has been produced)
then a remnant shall return. The return, as well as the
captivity, was part of God's purpose for his people.

4. A description of the ruler from Bethlehem as he reigns
over God's people.

stand and feed is a metaphor (so often used) from the work
of the shepherd—he shall feed God's flock.

they shall abide expresses the conviction, perhaps in the
very teeth of the evidence, that there would be no second

'fall of Jerusalem', but that the renewed life of Judah in Palestine would be perpetual.

he shall be great unto the ends of the earth indicates the expectation of the great king's universal empire.

5. Even when the new state is attacked the new king will be able to preserve peace. The use of the word 'Assyrians' is a clever device which links the prophecies of the historic Micah with the situation of a later day. In the OT 'Assyrians' stands for Babylonians (Lam. 5.6), Persians (Ezra 6.22) and Greeks (Zech. 10.10), much as Babylon stands for Rome in the Book of the Revelation. The contemporary crisis which the post-exilic writer is confronting is probably one concerned with Syria and the Seleucid kings, for instance, the conquest of Palestine by Antiochus III between 218 and 198 BC.

seven shepherds are a perfect number of guardians (shepherds).

eight princes are a more than perfect number of rulers; the phrases may refer in this ideal way to a coalition of governors who assumed leadership at that time.

6. The leaders will not only free Palestine, but go on to subjugate the invaders' own land.

the land of Nimrod is, as references show (cf. Gen. 10.8-11; I Chron. 1.10), the whole Babylonian-Assyrian Empire. The warrior-king will show that the most successful defence is a devastating, all-conquering offensive.

THE IDEAL FUTURE

5.7-15

There is some tension, if not contradiction, in this section, as between the pacific expectations of vv. 10-15 and the militarist ambitions of vv. 8 f. Yet the use of almost the same opening for vv. 7 and 8 is clearly meant to connect the two themes. It is probable that the verses are of diverse origin, but the compiler of the section and the editor of the book evidently saw some unity. It may be that the unity lies in the vision of a restored Israel living at peace with the nations, and bringing to them the blessings of her own knowledge and experience of God (vv. 7, 9-13) even though it was recognized that such an Israel could not come about save by some hard and costly military endeavour. This was certainly a dialectical movement of thought which many Jews underwent in the Maccabean period.

7. Here we have the ideal, peaceful future in its most general form. The remnant of Israel will dwell happily amongst the nations bringing them all a blessing in her religion (AS A DEW FROM THE LORD), but we must take special note of the fact that the latter half of the verse emphasizes that such a state will be the result of divine action and initiative (TARRIETH NOT FOR MAN).

8. This verse breathes a different air. Here Israel is like a lion among sheep, and when the lion moves the sheep suffer.

9. Here is the same idea with a different metaphor—that

of a fighting warrior with raised sword demolishing all his
enemies.

10-14. In the ideal future, however established, Israel's life
and service to God will be purified. There will be disarmament (I WILL CUT OFF THY HORSES . . . I WILL DES-
TROY THY CHARIOTS) to obviate trust being placed
improperly in arms (v. 10); there will be a demilitarization
with no more fortified towns (=cities) to remove the false
security they may evoke (v. 11); occultism will be abolished
and with it the pretence that any power other than God
controls men's lives (v. 12). All idols will be destroyed
and all places of idolatrous worship (vv. 13 f.). Israel's life
will rest solely in God, and derive wholly from him.

15. Here we are given, as it were, the other side of the
picture. If all the evil is to be taken from Israel, what of
the heathen nations? They too, will have to undergo the
purging fury of God. This verse may have been born in
bitter hatred of the Gentiles; even here its use retains
elements that need purifying. But it has an element of final
truth—that neither Jew nor Gentile, neither Christian nor
non-Christian can come into the final blessedness of God's
kingdom without costly and painful purification.

IV

WHAT GOD REQUIRES

6.1-8

GOD'S CONTROVERSY WITH HIS
PEOPLE

6.1-5

In this section the prophet adopts a popular and persistent metaphor to portray God's dealings with his people. The verses could well have come from the monarchical period, and we may well think of them as from Micah himself. The figure is that of the law court. God is about to open the case for the prosecution (he HATH A CONTROVERSY WITH HIS PEOPLE, AND HE WILL PLEAD—in the legal sense—WITH ISRAEL). The 'court' is the whole of nature—from the depths of the earth at its foundations to the very tops of the mountains. As a prelude to the indictment the prophet recalls what God has already done. He has done her no wrong, but rather delivered her from Egypt and its slavery, and sent her leaders. Miriam is the only woman mentioned here as one of the great figures (was she a heroine to Micah?). Micah then begins to recall all that God had done. He mentions Balak and Balaam, but gets no further.

TRUE RELIGION AND UNDEFILED

6.6-8

Instead Micah turns, wholly in the spirit of Amos, to remind his hearers that the mere existence and elaboration of ritual may beget 'religiosity' but it cannot please God.

To COME BEFORE God was a technical term used in sacrificial religion. How shall a man gain God's presence and enjoy his communion. Can it be bought with burnt offerings, with the sacrifice of young calves? Can ten thousand rams make an effective sacrifice to knit a man's soul to God—or tens of thousands of rivers of oil? Will it help a sinful man, who knows he is not worthy, to offer God his own first-born son in sacrifice? Will that lead God to admit man to the divine fellowship? Or, to put it in other words, can man deal with his bad conscience by expiatory sacrifices?

Micah's answer is plain and simple. What God asks of man is TO DO JUSTLY, TO LOVE MERCY, AND TO WALK HUMBLY WITH GOD. Like many simple statements it is profounder than it appears. Micah speaks to his fellow-Hebrews who have their own way, as they think, of securing God's favour, in terms that apply to man as man. There are no special terms for Jews; God deals with all as men. Moreover it is plain that for any man God's favour will not be won or lost by zeal, or lack of it, for religious rites; God's favour will be lost by injustice, by ruthlessness, by pride, and made possible by justice, mercy and humility. Justice is the maintenance of proper and honest relationships with one's fellows, not simply the ordering of them in a court of law; TO LOVE MERCY is to love good-will, not to be one

who enjoys nursing a grievance or harbouring revenge;
TO WALK HUMBLY WITH GOD is to be content with what his
will disposes, to be ready to learn from him and submit to
his guidance. It thus appears that virtue is not an end in
itself, but the very basis and means of our communion with
God; and that communion with God is not something un-
related to our characters and daily life, but something
bound up with its intention and quality. In this verse Micah
really anticipates the summary of religion that Jesus himself made in Matt. 22.34-40.

V

JUDGMENT AND HOPE

6.9–7.20

THE NEMESIS OF DISHONESTY

6.9-16

9. The prophet offers his own preface to what God is about to tell Jerusalem in face of some impending calamity. He knows that THE MAN OF WISDOM will recognize in the discomforting words the inevitable actions of God against Jerusalem's sin. That is, the wise man will discern God's nature or NAME in the prophecy of doom, i.e., will recognize it as truly a word from God. Jerusalem is charged to HEAR THE ROD, i.e., to learn the lessons of her disasters (cf. Isa. 10.5, O ASSYRIAN, THE ROD OF MINE ANGER!) and to remember who appointed them, i.e., God.

10-15. Micah, much in the spirit of Amos, exposes the corrupt commerce of Jerusalem traders: TREASURES OF WICKEDNESS, fortunes made by dishonest practices; SCANT MEASURE, measuring vessels giving short measures (the 'lean ephah'—a 'short pint'); wicked balances, which favoured the tradesman against the customer; and deceitful weights, light for selling, and over-weight for buying. But the evil is not primarily in things, but is only exemplified in them. The root of evil is in men, FOR THE RICH MEN ARE FULL OF VIOLENCE, AND THE INHABITANTS HAVE SPOKEN LIES, AND

THEIR TONGUE IS DECEITFUL IN THEIR MOUTH (cf. Micah
3.1-3, where the evils are also denounced). God cannot let
such iniquity go unpunished: he will smite the city and
leave it desolate. The wicked traders will not be allowed to
enjoy their evil gains. Their food will not satisfy them, their
country will be overrun, even at its centre in Jerusalem
(THY CASTING DOWN SHALL BE IN THE MIDST OF THEE); they
will be unable to defend their property against the invader;
and if they manage to rescue some of it, it will only be for
a time (v. 14). All this will happen, declared Micah, between
one seed time and the following harvest (v. 15).

16. The evils are traced to their source. The practices Micah
complains of are not ' native' to his land. He sees them as
' imports' from the northern kingdom, whose sharp commercial practices the Judaean merchants have enviously
copied. But even that is not the last word, for the mal-
practices of Israel, as Amos had pointed out, were in the
last analysis due to the false religion of the people. In these
ways Judaea had become thoroughly ' commercialized'; she
would have to bear the burden of God's loving judgment.

THE FEARFUL CONTAGION OF EVIL

7.1-6

Here, like Abraham before him (Gen. 18.23 ff.) and Jeremiah after him (Jer. 5.1) Micah tries to find in the corrupt
society of his day an example of an upright and honest
man. His search is like that of a man who goes into the
vineyard after the vintage in the hope that some grapes will
have been missed. But none have. Just so, there are no
righteous men left. THE GOOD MAN IS PERISHED OUT OF THE

EARTH. In so corrupt a society everyone's virtue is tainted.

The shocking evil is that men hunt each other, as if they were legitimate prey. The rulers 'sell' men for bribes, and the judges do the same (3). The MISCHIEVOUS DESIRE of the great man is his desire for a 'rake off'. All this is WRAPPED UP in the pretence of administering justice and preserving equity. But the offence is known for what it is (A BRIER) to God, and the nemesis of injustice cannot be avoided for ever in his world.

Micah then gives a picture of the way in which such social corruption corrodes even the sanctities of family intimacy. It is folly to trust a friend in a society where everything—and everybody—has a price; nor could any advice offered to one be free from taint of suspicion—it *might* be offered for ulterior reasons; the dreadful disease could even get inside a family and turn sons against fathers, daughters against mothers. A purely materialistic evaluation of life and persons is bound to lead to this. (It is interesting to remember that Jesus cited these words from Micah to describe the sort of disturbance his own restoration of the good society would produce!).

THE UNCONQUERABLE HOPE

7.7-20

In the circumstances of the corrupt society that Micah has described, there is but one thing left for the man of God— to look to God for the humanly impossible deliverance (v. 7).

If vv. 8 ff. be from Micah, they are addressed to the enemy he foresees as about to conquer Judah; it is not impossible to suppose that such thoughts as these originated with

Micah himself. On the other hand, these might well be Micah-like oracles uttered by some later disciple at the time of the exile and directed to the Babylonian captors.

Micah (and/or his disciple) is convinced that when the inevitable doom comes, it will not be final (v. 8). In the darkness of that day God will be a light.

9. This expresses a characteristically biblical idea that the nation, and the individual, has sinned and deserved the retribution which God has sent, and yet that, in spite of the retribution, God would not, could not, being God, let his divine purpose be frustrated by the sin he had to punish. I SHALL BEHOLD HIS RIGHTEOUSNESS means 'see the vindication of all that he has done in the actual achievement of his purposes'.

When the day of such fulfilment comes, God's people will, of course, have place in it. Then the nation that conquered her, and thought the victory meant that the God of Judah was absent or impotent or non-existent, would realize that God was the real victor. The one-time conqueror would in turn be defeated. (It is instructive to compare this with Isa. 53, where a prophet of the exile sees Babylon and the nations coming to confess that what they had thought was Israel's God smiting his people and afflicting them was really nothing more than the savage triumph of their own ruthlessness: HE WAS BRUISED FOR OUR INIQUITIES . . . BY HIS STRIPES WE ARE HEALED.)

11 f. The prophet foresees a restoration of the city after the ravages of war. In its present form it might well apply to the hope of the return from exile, but equally there can be no urgent reason for supposing that Micah could not conceive of God's purpose for his people continuing through

and beyond a disaster. If DECREE is to be interpreted of
Micah we must suppose him to think of God rescinding his
decree of conquest and destruction for his people and
'removing it far'; if of the exile, then the reference will be
to Nebuchadnezzar's decree of total destruction. The restoration will not be only of buildings destroyed, but of
people removed. HE SHALL COME FROM ASSYRIA, i.e., the
land where the northern kingdom had been led captive.

12. the river is probably the Euphrates, and the sense of the
whole verse is that from wherever Jews had been scattered
they would, in the great time of restoration, return home.

13. But their return will be to a land bearing the marks
of the disaster that had befallen it, a constant reminder
of the unfaithfulness that occasioned it, and a spur to new
fidelity in the future. An alternative suggestion is that the
land in question is that of the surrounding tribes, so that
the restored Israel would live in a fertile land, and her one-
time conquerors in devastated territory.

14-17. The figure now changes to the shepherd and to pastoral life. The prophet prays to God (and his prayer in
accordance with God's will and word is effective) to come
and feed his people with his rod, i.e., his rule. This is
one OT instance of the Good Shepherd. To DWELL SOLI-
TARILY is to be free from invasion or conquest. Carmel
means 'fruitful land'; Bashan and Gilead were not only
good pasturages, but symbols of the expansion of the
Hebrew empire under David. Such a restoration will be
accompanied, like the first settlement in Palestine, by
marvellous things (miracles) as at the Exodus (v. 15);
these will astonish the Gentile nations by their power,
so that they are rendered speechless, unable to listen to

anything else than the great story of Israel's restoration
(THEY SHALL LAY THEIR HANDS UPON THEIR MOUTH, THEIR
EARS SHALL BE DEAF). They will be reduced to utter
abasement, and come from their fortresses (HOLES) in fear
and dread of the power of God.

18-20. In these final verses we possess the last comment on
the situation in which Micah stood, knowing man's wickedness, his nation's corruptness, the Gentiles' ruthlessness, and
the inevitable nemesis that all such wickedness was bound
to bring. It was bound to bring it because God's character
was greater than that of a punitive automaton keeping a
strict 'moral balance book'. The great wonder was that
God was one who pardons sin, and does not let retribution
go on for ever. His fundamental character is in his mercy,
however plain his judgments are. This being so, God's
people of Micah's age, of the age of the disciples who published his book, of any age, including our Christian age, can
be sure that beyond God's judgments lie his compassion, a
final destruction of evil within and without, so that the
people of God (pictured in v. 20 by the names of Jacob and
Abraham) will in the end find their true life in him.
Then the age-long purpose of God (WHICH THOU HAST
SWORN TO OUR FATHERS FROM THE DAYS OF OLD) will be
completed.

The Christian gospel consists in affirming that God has
so visited his people in his mercy and inaugurated that kingdom where his people DWELL SOLITARILY and are fed by
him. And even though the consummation of that kingdom
awaits a final end, it is a kingdom, begun in time, where
sin can be done away. God's mercy known and tasted, and
ETERNAL LIFE, become a present possession in BELIEVING ON
JESUS CHRIST WHOM GOD HATH SENT.

SHORT BIBLIOGRAPHY

The following are suggested for further reading. All are sound and scholarly; the Cambridge Bible aims at being simpler than the others. Both Westminster Commentaries are standard works.

On AMOS

R. S. Cripps, *A Critical and Exegetical Commentary on the Book of Amos*, Macmillan, 1929.

S. R. Driver, *The Books of Joel and Amos*, The Cambridge Bible for Schools, CUP, 1897.

E. A. Edghill, *Amos*, The Westminster Commentaries, Methuen, 1914.

W. Lüthi, *In the Time of Earthquake*, Hodder and Stoughton, 1940. A more theological and realistic commentary than most.

On MICAH

T. K. Cheyne, *Micah*, The Cambridge Bible for Schools, CUP, 1882.

G. W. Wade, *Micah, Obadiah, Joel and Jonah*, The Westminster Commentaries, Methuen, 1925.

On Both Books

G. A. Smith, *The Book of the Twelve Prophets*, Vol. I, new and revised edition, Hodder and Stoughton, 1928. An inspired and inspiring commentary.

The Interpreter's Bible, Vol. 6, Abingdon Press, Nashville, Tennessee, 1956.